Conquering Often Confused And Misspelled Words

Fifth Edition

Lawrence Scheg

This book belongs to :

Name: _____
Street: _____
City: _____ State: ____
Phone: _____

The information above is optional

R J Communications LLC
New York

In cooperation with

Sierra Publishing
San Francisco, California

ISBN: 0-9742756-3-8

Published by
R J Communications
51 East 42nd Street, Suite 1202
New York, NY 10017

In cooperation with
Sierra Publishing
1034 Emerald Bay Road
South Lake Tahoe, CA 96150-6200

Contact for Domestic and International Orders:
Send E-mail to: mailsierrapublishing@yahoo.com
or visit www.SierraPublishing.com

Printed in the United States of America
6th printing

How to Use the Enclosed CD Rom

Step 1: **Carefully** remove the CD from the CD pocket holder attached to the back cover.

Step 2: Insert the CD into your computer. Double click on "My Computer."

Step 3: Double click on the drive that contains the CD as indicated by a string of numbers following that drive letter. This will open the CD.

Step 4: Double click on each of the following folders to install the readers or other information contained within them:

      A. **Adobe Reader:** Double click on "Adobe Reader Installer." This installs the Adobe Reader which will let you view and print any enclosed Adobe files as indicated by PDF on the disk.

      B. **PowerPoint Reader:** Double click on the "PowerPoint Reader Installer" to install the PowerPoint Reader. Once opened, click on "pngsetup". Next, you will see a rectangular box with a flashing curser in it. Type the letters: PPR, then hit "Enter" on your keyboard. It will ask if you want to create this directory, answer "yes". It will now finish installing the PowerPoint Reader. This allows you to play the PowerPoint vocabulary games, and view the PowerPoint presentations. (If this does not load properly on your computer, you probably have missing files or need to perform a Disk Defragmentation)

The games on the CD will only run after the installation of the PowerPoint reader unless you have the PowerPoint program version 97 or higher running on your computer.

Word 2000 is needed to view and print most of the Word documents. Some Word documents might work with earlier versions of Word. **MS Works is <u>not</u> the same as MS Word and will not open or print these documents.**

      C. **Adobe E-Book Reader:** Install this into your computer and you will be able to view the entire workbook on your computer screen, instantly look up nearly any vocabulary word in the built in E-Book dictionary, highlight text, and other useful tasks. Once the E-Book Reader is installed, simply drag and drop the "Adobe E-Book Version of the workbook" file onto the open E-Book template and in just seconds you are ready for a journey into E-Book technology.

Codes:
      PDF = Adobe File
      W -A Word file
      PPT = PowerPoint created document

Please, do not scratch, dirty, or allow fingerprints to corrupt your CD. Handle with care and only by the edges or center opening. If CD malfunctions, clean with mild dish detergent and dry with a soft lint free cloth. If it still malfunctions, contact <u>ProfessorScheg@Yahoo.Com</u> for instructions on how to receive a replacement disk.

How to use the Audio Practice Tests

1. Put your disk into the CD drive of your computer.
2. Click on "My Computer" on your desktop.
3. You will now see "Disk1Scheg" or "Disk2Scheg" depending upon which disk you put in the drive.
4. Click on that disk.
5. When it opens, find the folder "Audio Practice Tests" and click on it.
6. Find the chapter or page number that corresponds to the words that you want to hear and click on that file.
7. The Audio Practice Tests will open in virtually any audio program that is installed on your computer.
8. You may now hear the words pronounced. You may "pause" the word dictation, "reverse" to repeat a word, or "play" as many times as you'd like.
9. The Audio Practice Tests may be used to learn the proper pronunciation of the words, or you may test yourself on their proper spelling. Simply write the words on a sheet of paper as they are dictated and then turn to the proper page (as directed at the end of each test) to correct your answers.
10. The audio practice tests may also be used with WebCt if your instructor has access to WebCt. Practice tests are available to all instructors who use WebCt.

Contents

Plus … The fifth edition contains puzzles, interactive puzzles on the CD Rom, "Rewrite Your Words" sheets, and "Most Commonly Used Definition" sheets that aid the student in mastering the words.

The i Before e Rule

Write i before e...	...except after c...	...or when sounded like a as in neighbor and weigh.
1. achieve	19. ceiling	26. eight
2. believe	20. conceit	27. feign
3. brief	21. conceive	28. freight
4. chief	22. deceive	29. heinous
5. field	23. perceive	30. neighbor
6. fiend	24. receipt	31. reign
7. friend	25. receive	32. rein
8. grief		33. reindeer
9. hygiene		34. sleigh
10. niece		35. neigh
11. piece		36. vein
12. priest		37. weigh
13. relief		38. weight
14. shield		
15. shriek		
16. siege		
17. thief		
18. yield		

Exceptions To The Rule

39. ancient	44. financier	49. leisure	54. sovereign
40. counterfeit	45. foreign	50. neither	55. sufficient
41. efficient	46. forfeit	51. science	56. weird
42. either	47. height	52. seize	
43. Fahrenheit	48. heir	53. sheik	

"Write i before e, except after c, or when sounded like a as in neighbor and weigh."

This jingle is very useful when spelling words with the *ee* and *a* sounds but it does not apply to words with other sounds. The exercises that follow will enable you to apply this rule and recognize the exceptions.

    I.   Most words with the *ee* sound are spelled with the *i* before the *e*.
            Write each word three times in the space provided.

1. achieve	
2. believe	
3. brief	
4. chief	
5. field	
6. fiend	
7. yield	
8. grief	
9. hygiene	
10. niece	
11. piece	
12. priest	
13. relief	
14. shield	
15. shriek	
16. siege	
17. thief	

II. We usually put *i* before *e* if the sound is *ee*.
Complete the sentences below and apply the rule you just learned.

1. We can all **ach___ve** greatness if we try.

2. You should always **bel___ve** in yourself.

3. A **br___f** description should be short.

4. The **ch___f** of police has a large responsibility.

5. To declare a major is to decide on a **f___ld** of study.

6. A villain is a **f___nd,** or a criminal.

7. Study daily to avoid **gr___f.**

8. Doctors recommend good **hyg___ne** for good health.

9. My sister's daughter is my **n___ce.**

10. The word **p___ce** has pie in it.

11. The **pr___st** belongs to a church.

12. Some medicines can provide pain **rel___f.**

13. The knight wore a **sh___ld** for protection.

14. Some alarms let out a loud **shr___k.**

15. The castle was laid **s___ge** to by its enemy.

16. To be a **th___f** is to steal.

17. Recipes will **y___ld** a specified number of servings.

III. Fill in the blanks.

1. Write ___ before ___ except after ___ or when sounded like ___ as in n___ghbor and w___gh.

2. We usually put ___ before ___ if the sound is *ee.*

IV. If the sound is *ee,* but it follows a *c,* the *e* comes before *i.*
    CEI is a combination that is useful to memorize.
    Write the **cei** combination 10 times in the space provided below.

cei	_____ _____ _____

V. Use what you have learned about the **cei** combination to complete the sentences below.

1. The **c___ling** is over your head while indoors.

2. To feel superior is to behave with **conc___t**.

3. To have an idea is to **conc___ve** of something.

4. What a tangled web we weave when first we practice to **dec___ve**.

5. To **perc___ve** is to become aware of something.

6. If you make a purchase you should obtain a **rec___pt**.

7.   It is far better to give than to **rec___ve**.

VI. Write each of the words below in full.

1. ach—ve		7. bel--ve	
2. c--ling		8. conc—t	
3. ch--f		9. dec—ve	
4. perc--ve		10. p—ce	
5. rec--pt		11. rec—ve	
6. s--ge		12. y—ld	

VII. When pronounced correctly some words produce the *a* sound with the *ei* combination. Write each of the words below 3 times in the space provided.

1. eight	
2. feign	
3. freight	
4. heinous	
5. neighbor	
6. reign	
7. rein	
8. reindeer	
9. sleigh	
10. veil	
11. vein	
12. weigh	
13. weight	

VIII. Complete the sentences below. Remember to listen for the *a* sound.

1. The number following seven is ___**ght.**

2. If you pretend to be sick you **f___gn** an illness.

3. Trains move **fr___ght** from one location to the next.

4. A **h___nous** crime was reported to the police.

5. My **n___ghbor** is a close friend of mine.

6. The **r___gn** of a leader is the time they spend in power.

7. A horse's **r___n** is a leather strap.

8. An arctic animal with antlers is called a **r___ndeer.**

9. A **sl___gh** can be pulled by various kinds of animals.

10. A thin **v___l** was draped over the bride's face.

11. The nurse might examine your **v___n** for an injection.

12. A scale is used to **w___gh** things.

13. Numbers are used to declare **w___ght.**

Quiz

IX. Proofread the paragraph below. Rewrite any misspelled words.

When I was a child, my neighbor told her neice and me a story about Santa Claus that was hard for me to beleive. She said that one evening, while walking through a field, she saw something in the sky. It was a sliegh being pulled by eight tiny riendeer.

As with every rule there are exceptions to even this useful one. The jingle we have been practicing only applies to words with the *ee* or *a* sounds. In the words that follow, the sound of the word affects its spelling. Proper pronunciation is extremely important to spelling these words correctly.

X. Say each word aloud while you copy and memorize these exceptions to the rule. Listen carefully to the *ie/ei* combinations.

1. ancient		10. Fahrenheit	
2. counterfeit		11. financier	
3. efficient		12. foreign	
4. either		13. forfeit	
5. height		14. seize	
6. weird		15. sheik	
7. leisure		16. sovereign	
8. neither		17. sufficient	
9. science			

XI. Complete the sentences below. Decide between *ie/ei*.

1. If something is very old, it is **anc___nt**.

2. Fake money is considered **counterf___t**.

3. To manage your time well is to be **effic___nt**.

4. **___ther** you will succeed, or you should try again.

5. The temperature was 105 degrees **Fahrenh___t.**

6. When I consult my **financ___r,** I ask questions about money.

7. The import store sold many things from **for___gn** countries.

8. If you do not have enough players, you will have to **forf___t** the game.

9. My **h___ght** is measured in feet and inches.

10. My child is **h___r** to my fortune.

11. To relax is to have **l___sure** time.

12. If **n___ther** option is appealing, choose none of the above.

13. There are many fields of **sc___nce** to study.

14. The guards were ordered to **s___ze** the offender.

15. The **sh___k** is the leader of the Arab people.

16. This **sover___gn** nation is our home.

17. Ten dollars for gasoline should be **suffic___nt**.

18. Some words are spelled really **w___rd.**

Review Test—Chapter One

XII. Decide *ie/ei* then write each word in full in the space provided.

1. ach—ve		26. n—ce	
2. anc—nt		27. perc—ve	
3. bel—ve		28. p—ce	
4. c—ling		29. pr—st	
5. ch—f		30. rec—pt	
6. conc—t		31. rec—ve	
7. conc—ve		32. r—gn	
8. counterf—t		33. r—n	
9. dec—ve		34. rel—f	
10. effic—nt		35. sc—nce	
11. --ght		36. s—ze	
12. –ther		37. sh—k	
13. Fahrenh—t		38. sh—ld	
14. f—ld		39. shr—k	
15. f—nd		40. s—ge	
16. financ—r		41. sl—gh	
17. for—gn		42. sover—ign	
18. forf--t		43. suffic—nt	
19. fr—ght		44. th—f	
20. h—ght		45. v—l	
21. h—nous		46. v—n	
22. h—r		47. w- –gh	
23. l—sure		48. w—ght	
24. n—ghbor		49. w--rd	
25. n—ther		50. y—ld	

9

You will probably know most of the meanings for the words in this chapter, but write the definitions for those that are new to you. Additional copies of this form may be printed from the CD that came with this workbook.

Word	Most commonly used definition(s):

You will probably know most of the meanings for the words in this chapter, but write the definitions for those that are new to you. Additional copies of this form may be printed from the CD that came with this workbook.

Word	Most commonly used definition(s):

Rewrite your words

New word:	Practice writing the new word:		

Rewrite your words

New word:	Practice writing the new word:		

Across

5. head

7. lessen the pain

8. give in

11. accept

12. brother's daughter

13. a section of something

14. opposite of an enemy

15. protective piece of armor

Down

1. sadness

2. gain

3. place where crops grow

4. high pitched yell

6. cleanliness

9. forceful attack

10. villain

11. short time

13. church official

Chapter 01
Puzzle #2

Across

1. someone who finances

4. enough

6. one who inherits

7. to think of

10. measurement scale

12. to rule

14. one or the other

15. to take by force

16. to give up

17. blood vessel

Down

2. too much pride

3. animal's harness

4. sled drawn by horses

5. a fake copy, false

8. good use of time

9. a red nosed ____

10. to fake

11. not either

13. odd

Across

1. someone who finances
4. enough
6. one who inherits
7. to think of
10. measurement scale
12. to rule
14. one or the other
15. to take by force
16. to give up
17. blood vessel

Down

2. too much pride
3. animal's name s
4. sled drawn by horses
5. a fake copy; false
8. good use of time
9. a red nosed
10. to take
11. not either
13. odd

To Double
or
Not to
Double?

To double ...   **or**   **Not to double ...**

1. bit	1. bitten	1. bite	1. biting
2. fat	2. fatter	2. fate	2. fated
3. fib	3. fibber	3. dine	3. dining
4. fin	4. finned	4. fine	4. fined
5. grip	5. gripped	5. gripe	5. griped
6. hop	6. hopped	6. hope	6. hoped
7. mop	7. mopped	7. mope	7. moped
8. pin	8. pinned	8. pine	8. pined
9. plan	9. planned	9. plane	9. planed
10. rid	10. ridding	10. ride	10. riding
11. scrap	11. scrapped	11. scrape	11. scraped
12. shin	12. shinned	12. shine	12. shined
13. snip	13. snipped	13. snipe	13. sniped, sniper
14. strip	14. stripped	14. stripe	14. striped
15. tap	15. tapping, tapped	15. tape	15. taped, taping
16. win	16. winning	16. wine	16. wined

This Chapter addresses one of the most common spelling challenges – knowing when to drop a vowel, or double a consonant, (before adding an ending) and when not to do so. The simple exercises in this chapter should help you to understand the rules for doubling, and apply them correctly.

A good rule that works most of the time is: If the word ends in a consonant, you should double that consonant and add the ending (ed, ing, en, er). If the word ends in a vowel, you should drop the vowel and add the ending (ed, ing, en, er).

Another method for determining whether to double or not is determined by the **long** or **short** vowel sounds.

The vowels – a, e, i, o, u – can produce different sounds depending on their placement in a word. A **long** vowel is produced in words like **bite, fate, hope, mope,** and **tape.** In these words, we can hear the **long** vowel sound, for when we pronounce these words correctly, we can hear the long sound of the vowels: a sounds like a, o sounds like o, and so forth.

A **short** vowel sound is produced in words like **bit, fat, hop, mop,** and **tap.**
From this example, we can see that any sound that a vowel can make, that is not the actual sound of its name, is a **short** vowel sound.

I. Determine if the following words have **long** or **short** vowel sounds. Write **long** or **short** in the space provided.

1. bite		16. pin	
2. bit		17. ride	
3. dine		18. rid	
4. din		19. scrape	
5. fate		20. scrap	
6. fat		21. shine	
7. fine		22. shin	
8. fin		23. snipe	
9. gripe		24. snip	
10. grip		25. stripe	
11. hope		26. strip	
12. hop		27. tape	
13. mope		28. tap	
14. mop		29. wine	
15. pine		30. win	

In the exercise above, we can see that when a word ends with *e* , the vowel has to say its name and produces a _____ (long/short) vowel sound.

Now that we know the difference between **long** and **short** vowel sounds we are ready to learn the rules for doubling consonants.

We **do not double** a consonant when we hear the **long** vowel sound in a word.

We **do double** a consonant when we hear the **short** vowel sound in a word.

An easy way to remember this rule is to look at the root word. If the root word ends with an *e* the consonant **cannot** be doubled. If the root word ends with a *consonant* then doubling of the final consonant is usually required.

II. Determine if the words below have a **long** or **short** vowel sound.

1. biter		11. moped	
2. bitter		12. mopped	
3. coma		13. pining	
4. comma		14. pinning	
5. diner		15. riding	
6. dinner		16. ridding	
7. fiber		17. scraped	
8. fibber		18. scrapped	
9. hoping		19. taping	
10. hopping		20. tapping	

III. Decide to double or not to double in the sentences below.

1. I was not _____ (bit—en) by the dog although he is known to be a _____ (bit—er) and is often _____ (bit—ing) people.

2. We all had a nice _____ (din—er) while _____ (din—ing) at the _____ (din—er).

3. The _____ (fat—ed) pig was _____ (fat—ed) to be the main course of the huge feast.

4. The fisherman was _____ (fin—ed) by the authorities for catching the _____ (fin—ed) creature without a fishing license.

5. The patient was _____ (grip—ing) loudly about the long line in the Emergency room..

6. The children were _____ (hop—ing) that the Easter Bunny would be _____ (hop—ing) along soon.

7. The maid _____ (mop—ed) sadly when she saw the floor she had just _____ (mop—ed) was tracked with muddy footprints.

8. The carpenter was _____ (plan—ing) to do some _____ (plan—ing) on the door he was about to hang.

9. The cowboy was _____ (rid—ing) a horse while _____ (rid—ing) the countryside of bandits and other outlaws.

10. After the car accident the metal was so badly _____ (scrap—ed) that the insurance company _____ (scrap—ed) the car by sending it to the wrecking yard.

11. The hungry little boy began _____ (shin—ing) up the tree to pick the _____ (shin—ing) red apple from the very top branch.

12. The _____ (snip—er) took aim at the man brandishing the _____ (snip—er) as a weapon.

13. She _____ (strip—ed) off her dress when she saw that it had been _____ (strip—ed) with wet paint.

14. The team celebrated _____ (win—ing) by _____ (win—ing) and dining the night away.

15. Smiling, he sat at his desk, _____ (writ—ing) the first letter he had ever _____ (writ—en).

You will probably know most of the meanings for the words in this chapter, but write the definitions for those that are new to you. Additional copies of this form may be printed from the CD that came with this workbook.

Word	Most commonly used definition(s):

You will probably know most of the meanings for the words in this chapter, but write the definitions for those that are new to you. Additional copies of this form may be printed from the CD that came with this workbook.

Word	Most commonly used definition(s):

Rewrite your words

New word:	Practice writing the new word:		

Rewrite your words

New word:		Practice writing the new word:	

Chapter 02

Across

2. act of taking a ride

4. wished for

6. cut off a rose

8. one who secretly shoots at

9. stuck with pins

12. more fat than

15. was ____ by a bee

16. opposite of losing

17. cleaned floor with a mop

Down

1. depressed state of hanging out

2. doing away with

3. bran in diet

4. the rabbit ____

5. complained

6. threw away

7. made plans

10. eating diner

11. teller of "white lies"

12. destined for

13. one who bites

14. financial penalty

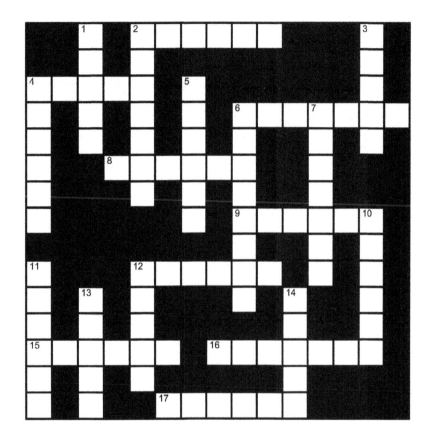

Just add s

In this chapter we will begin to pluralize nouns the simplest way that it can be done - by just adding s. To begin, we must first understand that a noun is a person, place, thing or an idea. These words are capable of being singular (meaning only one) or plural (meaning more than one.)

To form the plural of most nouns we simply add s to the end of the word. However, when forming the plural of some words that end with o, it is important that we memorize the exceptions to the just add s rule. With some words it is necessary to add es to form the plural. To further complicate the matter, some words may form their plural form by adding either s or es.

Just add s

1. arguments	7. gifts	13. originators	19. teachers
2. bracelets	8. helicopters	14. pearls	20. umbrellas
3. combs	9. ideas	15. pencils	21. vacuums
4. doctors	10. jokers	16. raisins	22. windows
5. elephants	11. lawyers	17. schedules	23. years
6. automobiles	12. noodles	18. slums	24. zebras

Ends with o, and just adds s

25. silos	29. dynamos	33. solos	37. radios
26. trios	30. egos	34. sopranos	38. ratios
27. cellos	31. embryos	35. patios	39. rodeos
28. curios	32. igloos	36. pianos	40. scenarios

Ends with o and adds es

41. vetoes	44. heroes	47. torpedoes
42. echoes	45. potatoes	
43. embargoes	46. tomatoes	

Ends With o, and may add either s or oes

48. lassos or lassoes	51. tobaccos or tobaccoes	53. banjos or banjoes
49. zeros or zeroes	52. mementos or mementoes	54. buffalos or buffaloes
50. nos or noes		

There is no jingle or catchy rhyme to help you remember these exceptions to the just add *s* rule. You must try to **memorize** these words.

I. Rewrite the **singular nouns** below. Just add *s* to the end to form the **plural** of each word in the space provided.

1. argument		13. originator	
2. bracelet		14. pearl	
3. comb		15. pencil	
4. doctor		16. raisin	
5. elephant		17. schedule	
6. fool		18. slum	
7. gift		19. teacher	
8. helicopter		20. umbrella	
9. idea		21. vacuum	
10. joker		22. window	
11. lawyer		23. year	
12. noodle		24. zebra	

II. Complete the sentences below. Write the **plural noun** by adding *s* to the end of the **singular noun**.

1. The _____(teacher) want paper and _____(pencil) for the exam.

2. _____(Pearl), _____(bracelet) and _____(comb) are fun to play dress-up with.

3. Frightened _____(zebra) and _____(elephant) ran from the noisy _____(helicopter) which were landing in the wildlife reserve.

4. The _____(doctor) and _____(lawyer) had _____(argument) with each other about their _____(schedule).

5. The _____(fool) and _____(joker) had strange _____(idea) about what _____(gift) would be appropriate.

6. The _____(window) on the _____ (house) in the _____(slum) were boarded up for _____(year).

7. Children like to eat _____(noodle) and _____(raisin).

8. A soggy salesman was selling _____(vacuum), although he was wishing that he had _____(umbrella) for sale instead.

III. Add *s or es* to the end of each word below to form the **plural** of each word in the space provided. A few of these words may be spelled either way. **Put both spellings in the box when applicable.**

1. alto		12. piano	
2. banjo		13. radio	
3. cello		14. ratio	
4. curio		15. rodeo	
5. dynamo		16. scenario	
6. ego		17. silo	
7. embryo		18. solo	
8. igloo		19. soprano	
9. lasso		20. tobacco	
10. memento		21. trio	
11. patio		22. zero	

IV. Complete the sentences below. Write the **plural noun** by adding *s* to the singular noun. Some of these words can be spelled either way. Put a star above those words.

1. The musicians left all of their _____(cello), _____(banjo) and _____(piano) outside when both _____(patio) were flooded with fans.

2. Cheers rose up from the crowd as the _____(lasso) encircled the horns of the bull at one of the best _____(rodeo) in the state.

3. The _____(ego) of all the _____(alto) and _____(soprano) made them want to sing _____(solo).

4. All _____(tobacco) can affect the health of developing _____(embryo).

5. This comic book describes exciting _____(scenario) where the _____(dynamo) fight crime in _____(trio).

6. My Grandmother kept important_____(memento) in her cabinet with her _____(curio).

7. In Iowa, there are plenty of _____(silo), but _____(igloo) are easily counted by _____(zero).

Quiz
V. Form the **plural** of each noun.

1. alto		11. scenario	
2. argument		12. teacher	
3. bracelet		13. tobacco	
4. curio		14. trio	
5. dynamo		15. umbrella	
6. elephant		16. vacuum	
7. helicopter		17. window	
8. lawyer		18. year	
9. memento		19. zebra	
10. originator		20. zero	

To form the plural of **most** nouns we simply just add _____ .

The next exercise is meant to help you memorize a few exceptions to the just add *s* rule. These words must have *es* added to them to correctly form the **plural**.

VI. Rewrite the **singular nouns** below. Remember to add *es* to the ends of the words to form the **plural nouns**. Practice writing the **plural** form of the words at least three times in the space provided.

1. buffalo	
2. echo	
3. embargo	
4. hero	
5. no	
6. potato	
7. tomato	
8. torpedo	
9. veto	

VII. Complete the sentences below. Write the **plural noun** by adding *es* to the end of the **singular noun.**

1. Settlers contributed greatly to the disappearance of most of the _____ **(buffalo)**.

2. My ears were ringing as the hall was filled with the loud _____ **(echo)** of hundreds of bells.

3. Trade _____ **(embargo)** can cripple a nation's economy.

4. Police officers are often considered _____ **(hero)** by their communities.

5. I have never heard more _____ **(no)** from any other than my own mother.

6. Eating baked _____ **(potato)** is healthier without butter.

7. _____ **(Tomato)** are sometimes considered a fruit and other times a vegetable.

8. Submarines have been known to carry _____ **(torpedo)**.

9. Several _____ **(veto)** were enacted during the Governor's recent budget cuts.

Quiz

VIII. Fill in the blanks.

When forming the plural of most nouns we just add _____. There are a few exceptions to this rule, and with these words we must add _____ to form the plural.

Write the plural of each noun in the space provided.

1. alto		11. lasso	
2. banjo		12. memento	
3. buffalo		13. patio	
4. cello		14. piano	
5. curio		15. potato	
6. echo		16. radio	
7. embargo		17. scenario	
8. embryo		18. tomato	
9. hero		19. torpedo	
10. igloo		20. veto	

IX. Proofread the paragraph below. Rewrite any misspelled words.

The torpedos sank the enemy submarine. The strike was in response to the many embargos we had heard discussed on the radio. The few survivor were given a hero's welcome when they returned home. Now, several yeares have passed since the argument between the two nation first became an issue.

X. Fill in the blanks.

A **singular noun** is _____(only one/ more than one).

A **plural noun** is _____(only one/ more than one).

To form the **plural** of most nouns we simply add ___(s/es). Some exceptions require us to add _____(s/es) to form the **plural.**

XI. Write the plural of each noun in the space provided.

1. bracelet		11. lawyer	
2. buffalo		12. memento	
3. curio		13. no	
4. doctor		14. noodle	
5. echo		15. originator	
6. embargo		16. potato	
7. embryo		17. tomato	
8. helicopter		18.torpedo	
9. hero		19. veto	
10. idea		20. zero	

You will probably know most of the meanings for the words in this chapter, but write the definitions for those that are new to you. Additional copies of this form may be printed from the CD that came with this workbook.

Word	Most commonly used definition(s):

You will probably know most of the meanings for the words in this chapter, but write the definitions for those that are new to you. Additional copies of this form may be printed from the CD that came with this workbook.

Word	Most commonly used definition(s):

Rewrite your words

New word:		Practice writing the new word:		

Rewrite your words

New word:		Practice writing the new word:		

Chapter 03
Puzzle #1

Across

1. many wrapped presents

5. many collapsible shades for protecting against weather

6. medical professionals

10. dried grapes

12. drawing tools

13. designate for fixed times

15. people who rely on humor

16. passing time

Down

2. academic instructors

3. cars

4. used for cleaning carpets

7. poor areas

8. inspirational thoughts

9. dangling round objects on wrist

11. shaped pasta

14. toothed instruments for arranging the hair

Chapter 03
Puzzle #2

Across

1. many living things in the early stages of development

3. a group or set of more than three

5. ivory keyed instrument

6. bass instruments, rhymes with Jell-o

8. strange or rare objects

11. outdoor dining areas

13. degree between two or more numbers

14. electrical generators

15. more than one but singing alone

Down

1. many views of the self

2. people with the highest singing voices

4. cowboys, bulls, clowns traveling from town to town

7. many different outcomes

9. wireless transmission boxes

10. homes made of ice

12. storage places for grain

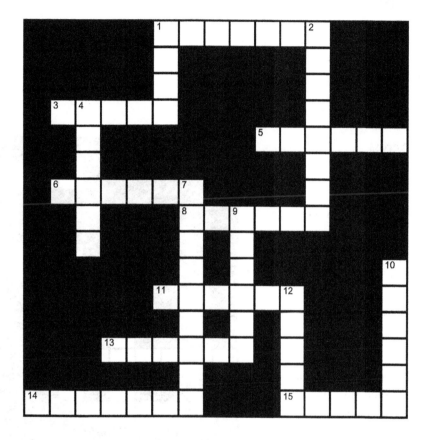

Chapter 03
Puzzle #3

Across

2. under water weapons

4. prohibitions on commerce

6. round, edible tropical herbs related to the potato

7. negative votes

Down

1. people who help others without regard for their own life

3. edible starchy tubers related to the tomato

4. repetitions of sounds

5. forbids, prohibits

Chapter 03
Puzzle #4

Across

3. stringed instruments similar to guitar but round at base & with 5 strings

6. favorite reminders

7. ropes used to corral horses

8. many 0's

9. plural of memento

Down

1. large wild bovine mammals

2. leaves used for smoking

3. plural of buffalo

4. musical instruments with long necks

5. plural of lasso

8. plural of zero

Across

3. stringed instruments similar to guitar but round at base & with 5 strings

6. favorite reminders

7. ropes used to corral horses

8. many 0's

9. plural of mercado

Down

1. large wild bovine mammals

2. leaves used for smoking

3. plural of buffalo

4. musical instruments with long necks

5. plural of lasso

8. plural of hero

Chapter 4

The Story of Stories & Other Noun Plurals

Ends with y and add s

1. alleys	4. donkeys	7. monkeys
2. **trays**	5. freeways	8. turkeys
3. nays	6. journeys	9. valleys

Change the y to i and add es

10. city	16. family	22. navy
11. cities	17. families	23. navies
12. country	18. lady	24. story
13. countries	19. ladies	25. stories
14. enemy	20. library	26. summary
15. enemies	21. libraries	27. summaries

Drop is and add es

28. analysis	34. hypothesis	40. synopsis
29. analyses	35. hypotheses	41. synopses
30. crisis	36. oasis	42. thesis
31. crises	37. oases	43. theses
32. diagnosis	38. parenthesis	44. neurosis
33. diagnoses	39. parentheses	45. neuroses

Forming the plural of most nouns is not a difficult task. In chapter three we learned how to just add *s* to the end of most nouns to form the plural. We also learned that some words must have *es* added to them to properly form the plural. This chapter focuses on words that end with *y* as well as words that end with *is*. In this chapter, we will practice just adding *s* as well as learning to change the ending of a word to form its plural.

1st Rule:

Forming the plural of words that end with *y* depends entirely on the letter that precedes the *y*. Words like *monkey* that end with *y*, and have a <u>vowel</u> preceding the *y*, only need *s* added to the end to form the plural.

I. Add *s* to the end of each word to form its plural. Notice that a **vowel** precedes the *y* at the end of each word. Practice writing the plural form of each word at least **three** times in the space provided below.

1. alley	
2. boy	
3. clay	
4. donkey	
5. freeway	
6. journey	
7. monkey	
8. tray	
9. valley	

2nd **Rule:**

Words like *family* that end with *y* and have a **consonant** preceding the *y,* must change the *y* to *i* before adding *es* to form the plural. Following this rule the word *family* becomes *families*.

II. Change the final *y* to *i* and add *es* to form the plural of each word. Notice that a **consonant** precedes the final *y* of each word. Practice writing the plural form of each word at least **three** times in the space provided below.

1. city	
2. country	
3. enemy	
4. family	
5. lady	
6. library	
7. navy	
8. story	
9. summary	

III. Complete the sentences below. Decide whether to just add *s,* or to change the *y to i,* and add *es* to form the plural of each word in the space provided below.

1. The _____(**boy**) all had _____(**family**) in different _____(**city**).

2. _____(**Library**) almost always have _____(**lady**) to tell wonderful _____(**story**) to the children who visit them.

3. _____(**Navy**) protect _____(**country**) from their _____(**enemy**).

4. Migrating _____(**monkey**) make _____(**journey**) over mountains and down into _____(**valley**).

5. The _____(**donkey**), of the peddlers, were used to transport the various _____(**clay**) that the ornate _____(**tray**) and vases were made from.

6. The city planning commission reviewed the _____(**summary**) detailing the condition of all the roads and _____(**alley**) within its limits, but left the _____(**freeway**) alone.

45

IV. Fill in the blanks.

1. When a word ends with a **vowel** before the final *y* we _____ **(do/do not)** drop the final *y* before making the word plural.

2. A **consonant** before the final *y* tells us that we _____ **(can/cannot)** just add *s* to make the word plural.

3. When we change *y* to *i* to make a word plural we must add_____ **(s / es)** to the end of the word.

3rd Rule: Forming Plurals by changing the ending is to es:

If we were to simply add *s* to words ending with *is* the plural of these words would no longer make sense. The pronunciation of words ending with *is* changes, when in their plural form, to sound like *es*. That is why we change *is* to *es* when forming the plural of the words. Note: Words ending in *sis* have the sound of sis in the word sister. Words ending in *ses* sound like seas or sees.

V. Change *is* to *es* to properly form the plural of each word. Practice writing the plural of each word at least three times in the space provided below.

1. analysis	
2. crisis	
3. diagnosis	
4. hypothesis	
5. neurosis	
6. oasis	
7. parenthesis	
8. synopsis	
9. thesis	

46

VI. Complete the sentences below. Remember to change *is* to *es* to form the plural of each word in the space provided.

1. Weary eyed, the professor reviewed all of the _____ **(analysis)** contained in the _____ **(thesis)** from her students.

2. On career day, the E.M.T.'s were very popular as they gave the students their _____ **(synopsis)** of the various _____ **(crisis)** they respond to.

3. In _____ **(parenthesis)** on the document were the various doctor's _____ **(diagnosis)** of the patient. They all stated that the subject suffered from various forms of _____ **(neurosis)**.

4. The children in school formed _____ **(hypothesis)** about how _____ **(oasis)** are formed in the desert.

Quiz

VII. Fill in the blanks.

1. If we just add *s* to the end of **analysis** to form its plural, the word _____ **(would/would not)** make sense.

2. To form the plural of a word ending with *is* we should _____ **(add** *s*/ change *is* to *es*)**.

47

VIII. Form the plural of each word in the space provided below.

1. analysis		6. family	
2. country		7. hypothesis	
3. diagnosis		8. library	
4. donkey		9. monkey	
5. enemy		10. summary	

Review Test—Chapter Four

IX. Proofread the paragraph below. Rewrite any misspelled words.

My favorite storys have always been about the brave men and womens who first

settled in America. I could not imagine enduring the hardshipes and triales that they

had to endure. I get upset at the local store for being out of my favorite ice cream.

How would I have fared if I had to hunt for, or grow, my own foods?

X. Fill in the blanks.

1. To form the plural of most words we simply add _____ *(s/ es)*.

2. Words that end with **y** and have a _____ **(vowel/consonant)** preceding the final **y** just add **s** to form the plural.

3. If a consonant precedes the final **y** then we must _____ **(drop/keep/ change the y to i** and add _____ *(s/es)*.

4. Words ending with **is** _____ **(can/cannot)** just add **s** to form their plural.

XI. Write the plural for each of the words in the space provided below.

1. alley		10. lady	
2. analysis		11. library	
3. clay		12. navy	
4. country		13. neurosis	
5. diagnosis		14. parenthesis	
6. enemy		15 story	
7. family		16. summary	
8. freeway		17. synopsis	
9. journey		18. thesis	

You will probably know most of the meanings for the words in this chapter, but write the definitions for those that are new to you. Additional copies of this form may be printed from the CD that came with this workbook.

Word	Most commonly used definition(s):

You will probably know most of the meanings for the words in this chapter, but write the definitions for those that are new to you. Additional copies of this form may be printed from the CD that came with this workbook.

Word	Most commonly used definition(s):

Rewrite your words

New word:	Practice writing the new word:		

Rewrite your words

New word:	Practice writing the new word:		

Across

1. more than one library

4. more than one donkey

8. more than one valley

9. adventures

10. not friends

11. more than one city

12. more than one summary

Down

1. opposite of the men's room

2. The building is several _____ high.

3. more than one family

5. more than one navy

6. more than one country

7. more than one monkey

54

Across

4. several informed opinions

5. green place in the desert

6. huge problems

7. more than one theory

10. more than one summary

12. quirk of the mind

13. (( ))

14. huge problem

15. educated critique of material

Down

1. theory

2. several quirks of the mind

3. more than one thesis

8. more than one green spot in the desert

9. more than one critique

10. a summary

11. main point of an article

More Noun Plurals

1st Rule:

We normally add *es* to words that end in ch, sh, x, z, or ss.

To form the plural of these words you need to listen carefully to the pronunciations of the plural form. A word like **arch** would not be easily pronounced with an *s* added to the end of it. The *es* combination provides the extra syllable needed for clarity when making this word plural. When we say the word **arches** we can hear the extra syllable at the end of the word that is produced by the *es* combination

1. arch	1. arches	8. ax	8. axes
2. boss	2. bosses	9. box	9. boxes
3. brush	3. brushes	10. business	10. businesses
4. church	4. churches	11. crutch	11. crutches
5. dish	5. dishes	12. glass	12. glasses
6. lash	6. lashes	13. princess	13. princesses
7. stitch	7. stitches	14. tax	14. taxes

I. Add *es* to the end of each word to form its plural. Listen for the extra syllable as you say the plural form of each word aloud. Practice writing the plural of each word at least three times in the space provided below.

1. arch	
2. ax	
3. boss	
4. box	
5. brush	
6. business	
7. church	
8. crutch	
9. dish	
10. glass	
11. lash	
12. princess	
13. stitch	
14. tax	

2nd Rule:

Words ending with *f*:

Words that end with the *f* sound form their plurals two different ways. Some words like **belief** just add *s*, i.e. **beliefs**. Other words like **knife** change the *f* to *v* and add *es*. For example *knife* changes to **knives**. The change in spelling can be heard when the plural form of the word is pronounced correctly.

To form the plural of a word like **chef** we should try saying the word aloud and listen to which form of the word sounds most clear. Would you say **chefs** or **cheves**? Clearly, **chefs** is more easily pronounced than **cheves**. A word like **elf** would become either **elfs** or **elves** in its plural form. After saying each word aloud **elves** seems more easily pronounced than **elfs**. This choice is not based on the spelling of the word but on its pronunciation. Familiarity with these words is what we need to accurately form their plural.

Ends with the *f* sound

1. belief	1. beliefs	8. knife	8. knives
2. calf	2. calves	9. leaf	9. leaves
3. chef	3. chefs	10. life	10. lives
4. elf	4. elves	11. loaf	11. loaves
5. grief	5. griefs	12. shelf	12. shelves
6. gulf	6. gulfs	13. thief	13. thieves
7. half	7. halves	14. wife	14. wives

II. Decide whether to add *s,* or to change the *f* to *v* and add *es,* to form the plurals of the words below. Listen carefully to the pronunciation of the plural of each word as you say them aloud. Practice writing the plural of each word at least three times in the space provided below.

1. belief	
2. calf	
3. chef	
4. elf	
5. grief	
6. gulf	
7. half	
8. knife	
9. leaf	
10. life	
11. loaf	
12. proof	
13. shelf	
14. thief	
15. wife	

Quick Quiz

III. We can determine how to form the plural of a word that ends with the *f* sound by its _____ (spelling/pronunciation).

IV. Form the plural of each word in the space provided below.

1. ax		7. leaf	
2. belief		8. princess	
3. business		9. proof	
4. crutch		10. stitch	
5. grief		11. thief	
6. knife		12. glass	

V. Complete the sentences below. Decide if you should add *s*, or change *f* to *v* and add *es*. Say each word aloud until you are familiar with the proper pronunciation for the plural of each word.

1. While visiting a historical little town we noticed that the _____ **(arch)** on the _____ **(church)** were far more elaborate than that of our church back home.

2. Some _____ **(wife)** have been known to break a few _____ **(glass)** while washing _____ **(dish).**

3. Happy little_____ **(calf)** spend their _____ **(life)** in lush green pastures.

4. While preparing a meal for the visiting _____ **(princess),** the nervous _____ **(chef)** realized that they needed sharper _____ **(knife)** to slice the _____ **(loaf)** of freshly baked bread.

5. Whether you need _____ **(stitch)** or _____ **(crutch),** the emergency hospital can help you 24 hours a day.

6. Many _____ **(business)** suffer from having too many _____ **(boss)** whose _____ **(belief)** differ greatly from each other.

7. The little girl's eyes sparkled like _____ **(topaz)** framed by long and wispy _____ **(lash).**

8. The _____ **(thief)** were very disappointed to find that the _____ **(box)** they had stolen were empty.

9. My grandmother told me a story about little _____ **(elf)** that use _____ **(ax)** to chop down trees in the forest.

10. The cemetery trees were shedding _____ (leaf) while the family expressed grief over their lost loved one.

11. Try to keep your _____ (tax) to a minimum by retaining all of your _____ (proof) for tax-deductible expenses.

12. Many _____ (gulf) are surrounded by tall _____ (cliff) whose other _____ (half) have been broken away by the oceans waves.

13. A bathroom may include _____ (shelf) to hold hair _____ (brush) or cosmetics.

Quick quiz

VI. Fill in the blank.

1. Words that end with the *f* sound can form their plural in _____ (one/two) ways.

VII. Decide if the statements below are true or false.

1. You can simply add *s* to the end of some words that end with the *f* sound to form their plural. _____ (true/false)

2. Some words that end with the *f* sound form their plural if you change the *f* to *v* and add *es*. _____ (true/false)

VIII. Form the plural for each word in the space provided below.

1. arch		9. elf	
2. belief		10. grief	
3. boss		11. half	
4. box		12. knife	
5. business		13. lash	
6. calf		14. proof	
7. church		15. shelf	
8. dish		16. thief	

You will probably know most of the meanings for the words in this chapter, but write the definitions for those that are new to you. Additional copies of this form may be printed from the CD that came with this workbook.

Word	Most commonly used definition(s):

You will probably know most of the meanings for the words in this chapter, but write the definitions for those that are new to you. Additional copies of this form may be printed from the CD that came with this workbook.

Word	Most commonly used definition(s):

Rewrite your words

New word:	Practice writing the new word:		

Rewrite your words

New word:		Practice writing the new word:		

Across

1. more than one gulf

4. golden _____

7. more than one calf

8. more than one thief

10. more than one business

12. The tree is full of _____.

14. more than one loaf of bread

15. more than one wife

16. more than one knife

17. The cut needed _____.

Down

2. more than one shelf

3. more than one life

4. cuts down trees

5. Broken legs need _____.

6. more than one princess

7. more than one chef

9. lots of sorrows

10. what you believe

11. One half plus one half equals two _____.

13. Santa's _____.

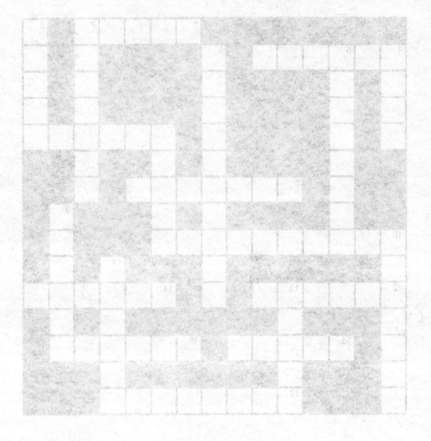

Chapter 06

Homonyms

These words sound the same but have different meanings

1. ascent /assent	21. grease / Greece
2. bare / bear	22. heal / heel
3. beach / beech	23. hoarse / horse
4. beat / beet	24. holey / holy/ wholly
5. board / bored	25. mantel / mantle
6. boarder / border	26. miner / minor
7. canvas /canvass	27. naval / navel
8. ceiling / sealing	28. peak / peek
9. cereal / serial	29. plain / plane
10. chord / cord	30. road / rode
11. cite / sight / site	31. sail / sale
12. coarse / course	32. scene / seen
13. dammed / damned	33. steal / steel
14. dear / deer	34. straight / strait
15. dew / do / due	35. to / too / two
16. dye/die and dyeing / dying	36. vain / vein / vane
17. fair / fare	37. waist / waste
18. flea / flee	38. weather / whether
19. flour / flower	39. wring / ring
20. foul / fowl	40. write / right / rite

A homonym is one of two, or more, words in the English language that have the same sound, but a different spelling and meaning.

The word *ascent* means to rise upward; *assent* means to agree.

Both of these words are pronounced the same, yet are spelled differently and have different meanings.

The above examples only represent a few homonyms. There are many more homonyms not listed here. The exercises in this chapter are meant to familiarize you with these words and their meanings.

I. Study the meanings of the *homonyms* below. Practice writing each word correctly in a sentence.

1. **ascent** — 1. to rise upward; 2. an upward slope

    _____

    assent — 1. to agree; 2. consent

    _____

2. **bare** — exposed, or without covering

    _____

    bear — 1. a large, clawed mammal; 2. to carry

    _____

3. **beach** — the shore of a body of water

    _____

    beech — a species of tree

    _____

4. **beat** — 1. to strike rhythmically or repeatedly; 2. (slang) being overly tired

    _____

    beet — a vegetable

    _____

5. **board** — a flat piece of sawed lumber or wood

    _____

    bored — 1. having been drilled to produce a hole; 2. a lack of interest

    _____

6. **boarder** — a paying guest

_____

border — the outer edge of something

_____

7. **canvas** — a heavy, closely woven fabric

_____

canvass — to completely cover or go through

_____

8. **ceiling** — the upper interior surface of a room

_____

sealing — 1. to apply a sealant; 2. shutting tight

_____

9. **cereal** — a food prepared from grains

_____

serial — 1. arranged in a series; 2. one of a series

_____

10. **chord** — three or more tones sounded harmoniously

_____

cord — a string of twisted strands or wires

_____

11. **cite** — 1. to quote as an example; 2. to summon before a court of law

_____

sight — to see

_____

site — a specific location

_____

12. **coarse** — rough or unfinished

_____

course — a route or a path

_____

13. **dammed** — held back (hint – from the word dam)

_____

damned — condemned, or doomed (hint – from the word damn)

_____

14. **dear** — highly esteemed

_____

deer – a wild hoofed mammal

_____

15. **dew** — moisture condensed from the air

_____

do — to bring about

_____

due — expected or scheduled

_____

72

16. **dyeing** — to color or stain (hint – from the word dye)

_____

dying — about to die (hint – from the word die)

_____

17. **fair** — 1. consistent, or equal; 2. livestock show; 3. pleasant; 4. of good
color or condition

_____

fare — 1. a fee charged; 2. an item for sale

_____

18. **flea** — a parasite

_____

flee — to runaway

_____

19. **flour** — powdered grain

_____

flower — the blossom of a plant

_____

20. **foul** — 1. offensive to the senses; 2. out of bounds

_____

fowl — a bird used as food

_____

II. Complete the sentences with the correct *homonym*.

1. The hunter was looking for _____ (dear/deer) when he stumbled across a _____ (bare/bear) unexpectedly.

2. The manager was on _____ (coarse/course) to the _____ (cite/sight/site) and _____ (dew/do/due) to arrive very soon.

3. Our tent had a strong _____ (canvas/canvass) roof so the _____ (ceiling / sealing) stayed nice and dry.

4. The petals of the _____ (flour/flower) were wet with the morning _____ (dew/do/due).

5. The chef prepared the _____ (foul/fowl) by rolling it in _____ (flour/flower).

III. Fill in the blanks with the correct *homonym*.

6. To see. _____ (cite/sight/site)

7. Rough or unrefined. _____ (coarse/course)

8. Condemned or doomed. _____ (dammed/damned)

9. To color. _____ (dyeing/dying)

10. Consistent or equal. _____ (fair/fare)

Across

2. Smokey the _____

3. rope

4. three notes sounded together

6. breakfast food

9. completely cover

10. type of tree often used for handles

12. closing

13. empty

14. no excitement

Down

1. climb upward

2. outer edge

3. top of room

5. sand & sea

7. renter

8. agreement

10. piece of lumber

11. linen material

12. one in a series

13. rhythm

14. red colored vegetable

Across

1. stopped up

3. condemned

5. edible bird

6. route

7. ground grain

8. parasite

9. doe

10. pass away

11. pleasant

13. rose

15. sweet

16. able to see

Down

1. payable now

2. morning moisture

4. color

5. not fair

6. to summon before a court

7. amount due

9. passing away

10. coloring

12. rough

13. run away

14. large work area

IV. Study the meanings of the *homonyms* below. Practice writing each word correctly in a sentence.

21. **grease** — a thick lubricant or oil

   _____

   Greece — a country in Southeastern Europe located on the Mediterranean Sea. (hint – Greek: both words have double ee)

   _____

22. **heal** — to restore to health, cure

   _____

   heel — 1. rear part of the foot; 2. to command a dog to stop and sit

   _____

23. **hoarse** — rough sound

   _____

   horse — a large hoofed mammal

   _____

24. **holey** — to be full of holes (hint – from the word hole)

   _____

   holy — associated with the divine or sacred

   _____

   wholly – completely, entirely (hint – from the word whole + ly, drop the e at the end of whole and add ly - which means in the manner of or in the way of …being wholc.)

   _____

25. **mantel (or mantle)** — 1. a shelf over a fireplace; 2. the facing around the fireplace

_____

mantle — 1. a sleeveless outer garment; 2. outer covering; 3. layer of earth between the crust and the core

_____

26. **miner** — an excavator, one who digs in the earth (hint: miner comes from the word mine. The suffix er means one who … – a miner is one who mines.)

_____

minor — 1. lesser in amount; 2. under legal age

_____

27. **naval** — 1. related to shipping; 2. related to the Navy

_____

navel — a mark on the abdomen of mammals ("belly button")

_____

28. **peak** — the highest point

_____

peek — to glance quickly

_____

29. **plain** — 1. free from obstruction; 2. open; 3. clear; 4. ordinary; 5. flat land

_____

plane — 1. an airplane; 2. flat surface (as in math usage)

_____

30. **road** — specified path for travel

_____

rode — past tense of ride

_____

31. **sail** — 1. fabric made for catching the wind; 2. to catch the wind; 3. riding on the wind or water; 4. driven by the wind; 5.move swiftly or effortlessly.

_____

sale — 1. exchange of goods or services for money; 2. selling goods or services at a lowered price.

_____

32. **scene** — the setting of an action

_____

seen — perceived with the eye

_____

33. **steal** — to take without permission

_____

steel — metal wrought from iron

_____

34. **straight** — free from curves

_____

strait — 1. a narrow waterway joining two larger bodies of water; 2. a tight place or situation; 3. to be confined.

_____

35. **to** — in the direction of

too — 1. the same as; 2. also

two — the number 2

36. **vain** — 1. effort without reward; 2. not modest

vein — a vessel through which blood returns to the heart

vane — a movable device that shows which way the wind is blowing

37. **waist** — the middle section of an object – especially when narrower than the rest of the object.

waste — 1. to use carelessly; 2. refuse, garbage

38. **weather** — the state of the atmosphere

whether — used to indicate a choice or an alternative

39. wring — to extract by twisting

_____

ring — 1. a circular object; 2. sound of a telephone

_____

40. write — to form letters or symbols on a surface

_____

right — 1. conforming to popular opinion; 2. correct; 3. opposite of left

_____

rite — 1. a solemn ceremony; 2. a customary ceremony or observance

_____

Quiz

V. Complete the sentences with the correct _homonym_.

1. The minister wore a _____(wholly/holey/holy) _____(mantel/mantle) while he attempted to _____(heal / heel) the sick child.

2. It would have been interesting to have _____(scene/seen) ancient _____(grease/Greece) for myself.

3. The cowboy _____(road/rode) his _____(hoarse/horse) _____(straight/strait) home after his work was finished.

4. The fisherman thought about how beautiful the _____(weather/whether) looked as he took a _____(peak/peek) up at his _____(sail/sale).

5. The _____(miner/minor) worked underground collecting iron ore for the _____(steal/steel) refinery.

6. A mark on the abdomen of mammals. _____(naval/navel)

7. A flat open piece of land is a _____. (plain/plane)

8. The same as, or also. _____(to/too/two)

9. Effort without reward. _____(vain/vein/vane)

10. Conforming to popular opinion; correct. _____(rite/right/write)

Review Test

A *homonym* is one of two or more words in the English language that _____(sound / mean) the same although they have different _____(sounds /meanings).

VI. Fill in the blanks:

1. The highest point. _____

2. In the direction of. _____

3. To form letters or symbols on a surface. _____

4. A circular object. _____

5. The state of the atmosphere. _____

6. To use carelessly. _____

7. An amount; the number 2. _____

8. To take without permission. _____

9. A vessel through which blood returns to the heart. _____

10. Free from curves. _____

11. Specified path for travel. _____

12. The setting of an action. _____

13. To see. _____

14. Rough or unfinished. _____

15. Expected or scheduled. _____

Across

4. entirely

6. country in the Mediterranean

7. less in importance

8. sacred

9. rough sounding voice

11. one who digs in the earth

14. past tense of ride

15. type of orange

16. It's a bird, it's a _____; no it's Superman!

17. cars ride on

Down

1. open fields

2. back of foot

3. glance

5. full of holes

6. thick oily substance

10. cowhands ride on

11. shelf over fireplace

12. related to the Navy

13. to get well

16. top of mountain

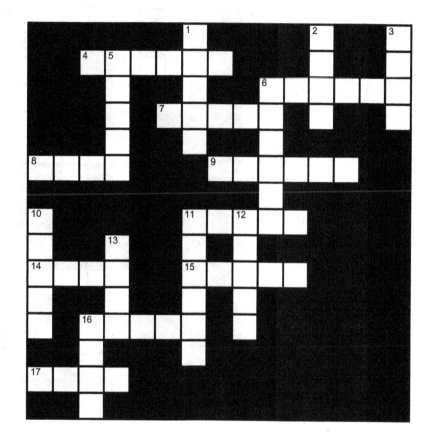

Across

2. twist

4. ceremony

5. blood flows through

8. atmospheric conditions

11. perceived with the eye

12. narrow passage

14. belt goes around

15. _____ of the crime

16. to take without permission

17. use a pen to _____

Down

1. boat that uses wind

2. choice

3. conceited

5. shows wind direction

6. mark down of prices

7. wedding band

9. 2

10. correct

11. no curves

12. tough metal

13. also

14. garbage

You will probably know most of the meanings for the words in this chapter, but write the definitions for those that are new to you. Additional copies of this form may be printed from the CD that came with this workbook.

Word	Most commonly used definition(s):

You will probably know most of the meanings for the words in this chapter, but write the definitions for those that are new to you. Additional copies of this form may be printed from the CD that came with this workbook.

Word	Most commonly used definition(s):

Rewrite your words

New word:		Practice writing the new word:		

Rewrite your words

New word:		Practice writing the new word:		

More Homonyms

They Sound the Same	
1. aisle / isle/ I'll	21. knew / new
2. a lot / allot	22. know / no
3. all ready / already	23. lessen / lesson
4. allowed / aloud	24. meat / meet
5. altar / alter	25. one / won
6. brake / break	26. pail / pale
7. buy / by / bye	27. passed / past
8. carat (also karat) / caret / carrot	28. peace / piece
9. close / clothes	29. pole / poll
10. complements / compliments	30. pore / pour
11. council / counsel	31. role / roll
12. desert / dessert	32. shone / shown
13. dual / duel	33. stake / steak
14. forth / fourth	34. stationary / stationery
15. forward / foreword	35. their / there / they're
16. hear / here	36. threw / through
17. hour / our	37. weak / week
18. its / it's	38. wear / where
19. lie / lye	39. cache / cash
20. wave / waive	40. might / mite

In chapter six we learned that a ***homonym*** is one of two, or more, words in the English language that have the same sound, but a different spelling and meaning. In this chapter we will work with more ***homonyms***.

I. Study the meanings of the *homonyms* below. Practice writing each word in a sentence.

1.   **aisle** — a path between rows

_____

    isle — an island

_____

    I'll – A contraction for *I will*

_____

2.   **a lot** — 1. opposite of a little; 2. much

_____

    allot — 1. to distribute by specified amount; 2. to allocate or give an allotment.

_____

3.   **all ready** — (all) the total number, (ready) prepared. (hint-all = everyone – everyone is ready/ all are ready)

_____

    already — 1. arrived at a specified time; 2. happened, occurred

_____

4.   **allowed** — permitted (hint-you allow something)

_____

    aloud — 1. with sound; 2. an audible tone; 3. can be heard

_____

5. **altar** – a sacred structure for ceremonies

---

alter – 1. to modify, 2. change

---

6. **brake** – 1. a stopping device; 2. to slow down

---

break — 1. to make unusable; 2. damage; 3. time off or time out; 4. to train (ex.-a horse)

---

7. **buy** – to acquire in exchange for money

---

by – 1. next to; 2. pass by

---

bye – 1. used to signify a departure; 2. farewell

---

8. **carat (also karat)** – a unit of weight for precious stones

---

caret – a mark used in proofreading.

---

carrot — an orange colored root vegetable

---

9. **close** – 1. to shut; 2. stop from being open

---

clothes – garments, articles of clothing

---

10. complements – that which completes. (hint: Complete and complement begin with the same 6 letters.)

_____

compliments – a form of praise; admiration. (hint: The difference in spelling between complement and compliment is the letter i. I compliment you.)

_____

11. council – an administrative assembly

_____

counsel – 1. an advisor; 2. advice; 3. instruction received; 4. advice received

_____

12. desert -to abandon

_____

dessert – a treat following a meal

_____

13. dual – two parts

_____

duel — pre-arranged formal combat

_____

14. forth — forward

_____

fourth – number four in a series

15. forward – in the direction in front of

_____

foreword – 1. an introductory note preceding the main text

_____

16. hear – to perceive sound

_____

here – in this place

_____

17. hour – 1. a unit of time; 2. sixty minutes

_____

our – the possessive form of we

_____

18. its – the possessive form of it

_____

it's — contraction of it is

_____

19. lie – 1. the opposite of the truth; 2. to recline

_____

lye — a strong alkaline solution

_____

20. wave – 1. to motion with the hand; 2. a curling of the water of an ocean or other body of water.

_____

waive — 1. to release; 2. to give up right or claim to something; 3. relinquish.

_____

II. Complete the sentences with the correct *homonym*.

1. _____(Our / Hour) baby is only ten months old and she can
   _____(all ready / already) say _____(buy / by / bye) when she
   leaves our neighbor's house..

2. _____(Its / It's) impossible to _____(altar / alter) your
   _____ (knew /new) _____ (close / clothes) in less than an
   _____ (hour / our).

3. The man walked _____(forward / foreword) onto the field as he prepared
   to have a _____(dual / duel).

4. You can only _____ (hear / here) something if it is said
   _____(allowed / aloud).

5. The one _____ (carat / caret / carrot) diamond ring was the perfect
   _____ (complement / compliment).

III. Fill in the blanks with the correct *homonym*.

1. An island. _____ (aisle / isle)

2. Possessive of it. _____ (its / it's)

3. An administrative assembly. _____ (council / counsel)

4. A treat following a meal. _____ (desert / dessert)

5. A stopping device. _____(brake / break)

Chapter 07
Words: 01-10

Across

3. an island

6. things you wear

7. to change

8. see you later

9. proof reading mark

11. it has happened

_____

12. everyone is ready

14. completes

15. bust

16. to purchase

Down

1. can be heard

2. The bride walked down the _____.

4. The groom waited at the _____.

5. unit of weight for precious stones

6. to shut

8. to stop

9. rabbits like this

10. to meter out

13. permitted

15. next to

Chapter 07
Words: 11-20

Across

1. administrative assembly

4. time - (one of twenty-four)

5. this place

7. fight between two persons

8. two similar items

9. strong alkaline substance

11. not true

12. words written at front of book

14. hot dry place

15. to motion with the hand

16. 4th

Down

1. to give advice

2. belongs to

3. go on

6. to listen

10. treat served with meal

12. going forward

13. give up right

17. belongs to us

IV. Study the meanings of the *homonyms* below. Practice writing each word in a sentence.

21. **knew** — prior knowledge; past tense of know

_____

new — unused

_____

22. **know** — present knowledge

_____

no — negative

_____

23. **lessen** — to make less, decrease

_____

lesson — something to be learned (hint-Son, learn your les<u>son</u>.)

_____

24. **meat** — the edible part of animals, nuts and fruits (hint-We eat m<u>eat</u>.)

_____

meet — to get together

_____

25. **one** — a single unit

_____

won — finished first

_____

26. pail — a watertight container with a handle

_____

pale —lacking color; whitish. (hint-Too much ale can make you p<u>ale</u>.)

_____

27. passed — past tense of pass; having gone by

_____

past — a time gone by (hint-remember: past, present, future)

_____

28. peace — without conflict

_____

piece — a portion of something (hint: A <u>pie</u>ce of pie.)

_____

29. pole — 1. a long slender piece of wood; 2. terminals on a battery; 3. North or South Pole

_____

poll — a survey (hint: persons doing polling usually have two legs = po<u>ll</u>)

_____

30. pore — a tiny opening

_____

pour — to cause to flow

31. role — a specific function or part

---

roll — 1. to move by repeatedly turning over; 2. a dinner roll, bun; 3. attendance roll.

---

32. shone — 1. past tense of shine; 2. reflected light (hint-You only have one letter different in sh<u>o</u>ne as compared to sh<u>i</u>ne from which it is derived.)

---

shown — 1. having been displayed; 2. past tense of show (hint-You can see the word show in <u>show</u>n.)

---

33. stake — 1. a post used for securing; 2. to secure

---

steak — a slice of meat

---

34. stationary — still, not moving (hint-The A in stationary looks like a person's legs when then they are standing very still. Draw a "stickman")

---

stationery — paper and envelopes used for letter writing (hint-The e in stationery can remind us of <u>e</u>nvelopes.)

---

35. their — possessive of they

there — in that place (hint-<u>here</u>, <u>there</u>, and everyw<u>here</u> are all places and all have <u>here</u> in them.)

they're — contraction for they are

36. threw — past tense of throw; tossed (hint only one letter difference between thr<u>o</u>w and thr<u>e</u>w.

through — 1. by way of; 2. in and out of something (hint-It's <u>rough</u> to go th<u>rough</u> some things.)

37. weak — lacking strength

week — seven consecutive days

38. wear — 1. to rub away, to erode; 2. to cover as with a piece of clothing

where — inquiry; in what place? (hint-indicates a place: <u>here</u>, t<u>here</u>, w<u>here</u> – all have <u>here</u> in their spellings.)

ware – Items of a similar kind (silverware, dinnerware, hardware, software)

39. cash — money in coins or bills

_____

cache — 1. a hidden supply of food or supplies; 2. a hiding place where a store of food or supplies are kept; 3. computer cache

_____

40. might — 1. strength; 2. power; 3. a chance that you will, maybe

_____

mite — 1. any of small insects belonging to the same class as the spider; 2. very small in size or amount (hint-A m<u>ite</u> can b<u>ite</u>.)

_____

Quiz

V. Complete the sentences with the correct *homonym*.

1. _____ **(Their / There / They're)** sure to _____**(know / no)** the answers after they complete the _____**(lessen / lesson)** this _____**(weak / week)**.

2. At the barbecue we _____**(threw / through)** _____**(stake / steak)** and other _____**(meat / meet)** on the grill.

3. After some time _____**(passed / past)**, the warring countries _____**(knew / new)** they wanted _____**(peace / piece)**.

4. Has anyone _____**(shone / shown)** the _____ **(knew / new)** secretary _____**(wear / where)** we keep the office _____**(stationary / stationery)**.

5. The sun _____**(shone / shown)** down on all the sunbathers and _____**(their / there / they're)** skin turned from _____**(pail / pale)** to golden tan.

101

VI. Fill in the blanks with the correct *homonym*.

1. I _____ (know /no) your brother from the tennis club.

2. The edible part of animals and fruit. _____ (meat / meet)

3. Without conflict. _____ (peace / piece)

4. A long slender piece of wood. _____ (pole / poll)

5. A tiny opening. _____ (pore / pour)

6. They tried to move the rock with all of their _____ (mite / might).

7. The soldiers had hidden a _____ (cash / cache) of weapons.

Review Test

VII. Fill in the blanks.

1. To distribute by specified amount. _____

2. Permissible. _____

3. To modify. _____

4. Next to. _____

5. A vegetable. _____

6. That which completes. _____

7. Prearranged formal combat. _____

8. An introductory note; before the text. _____

9. A unit of time; sixty minutes. _____

10. To get together. _____

102

11. A watertight container with a handle. _____

12. Past tense of pass. _____

13. A tiny opening. _____

14. Past tense of shine. _____

15. Still. _____

16. Possessive of they. _____

17. By way of. _____

18. Inquiry; in what place? _____

Chapter 07
Words: 21-30

Across

1. history

3. to ask questions

5. opening in the skin

7. lack of war

9. not used

11. something to be learned

13. 1

14. long slender piece of wood

15. to get together

Down

1. bucket

2. have knowledge of

3. section

4. make smaller

6. lack of color

7. gone by

8. had knowledge of

10. finished first

12. opposite of yes

14. to empty out a liquid

15. steak

Chapter 07
Words: 31-40

Across

2. strength

4. meat

5. It's _____ Mercedes.

6. having been displayed

7. slender pole

8. hidden supply

10. still, not moving

14. asking what place

15. function or part

16. not much strength

Down

1. to have on

2. very small insect

3. in and out

4. has shined

6. writing supplies

9. money

11. in that place

12. tumble

13. tossed

14. 7 days

You will probably know most of the meanings for the words in this chapter, but write the definitions for those that are new to you. Additional copies of this form may be printed from the CD that came with this workbook.

Word	Most commonly used definition(s):

You will probably know most of the meanings for the words in this chapter, but write the definitions for those that are new to you. Additional copies of this form may be printed from the CD that came with this workbook.

Word	Most commonly used definition(s):

Rewrite your words

New word: **Practice writing the new word:**

Rewrite your words

New word:	Practice writing the new word:		

Rewrite your words

New word:		Practice writing the new word:		

Rewrite your words

New word:		Practice writing the new word:		

118

To Keep or Drop the Final Silent e

A common spelling dilemma is in deciding to keep or drop the final silent e when adding a suffix to the end of a word. In this chapter we will learn the rules as well as the exceptions that help us make the right choice.

All of the spelling words in this lesson consist of a root word (that ends with silent e) and a suffix. In some words the silent e was kept, in others it was dropped. In most words this decision is based on the first letter of the suffix which is being added to the end of the word.

Examples:

use + ful = useful

      In this example the suffix, ful, begins with a consonant so the root word, use, keeps the silent e.

use + ing = using

In this example the suffix, ing, begins with a vowel so before adding this suffix to the same root word, use, we must drop the silent e.

Rule: With <u>most</u> words, we keep the silent e, if the suffix begins with a consonant. We drop the silent e, if the suffix begins with a vowel.

I. Circle the suffixes that begin with a consonant.

ing	ment	age	ful	able	ous	ly	ty	ite	dom

II. Circle the suffixes that begin with a vowel.

teen	ance	ion	ly	dom	ite	ous	able	age

These words change by dropping the 'e':

1. accuse
2. acknowledge
3. confuse
4. fame
5. have
6. judge
7. lose
8. love
9. oppose
10. oppose
11. ridicule
12. save
13. use
14. write
15. pore

1. accusing
2. acknowledgment (or -ement)
3. confusion
4. famous
5. having
6. judgment (or judgement)
7. losing
8. loving
9. opposing
10. opposite
11. ridiculous
12. saving
13. using
14. writing
15. porous

These words change by keeping the 'e':

16. definite
17. accurate
18. nine
19. nine
20. safe
21. sincere
22. state

16. definitely
17. accurately
18. nineteen
19. ninety
20. safety
21. sincerely
22. statement

These are <u>exceptions</u> to the rules above:

23. write
24. argue
25. nine
26. true
27. whole
28. wise
29. canoe
30. change
31. courage
32. dye
33. notice
34. outrage
35. peace
36. shoe
37. singe
38. toe
39. acre
40. mile

23. written
24. argument
25. ninth
26. truly
27. wholly
28. wisdom
29. canoeing
30. changeable
31. courageous
32. dyeing
33. noticeable
34. outrageous
35. peaceable
36. shoeing
37. singeing
38. toeing
39. acreage
40. mileage

114

III. Apply the rules you have just learned and combine the root words with the suffixes in the space provided below.

1. accurate + ly	
2. accuse + ing	
3. confuse + ion	
4. definite + ly	
5. fame + ous	
6. have + ing	
7. lose + ing	
8. love + ing	
9. nine + teen	
10. nine + ty	
11. oppose + ing	
12. oppose + ite	
13. ridicule + ous	
14. safe + ty	
15. save + ing	
16. sincere + ly	
17. state + ment	
18. use + ful	
19. use + ing	
20. write + ing	

IV. Fill in the blanks.

To add the suffix, **ty**, to the root word **safe** we _____ (drop / keep) the **silent** *e* because the suffix begins with a _____ (consonant / vowel). To add the suffix, **ing**, to the root word **save** we _____ (drop / keep) the **silent** *e* because the suffix begins with a _____ (consonant / vowel).

Exceptions to the Rule

Some exceptions to the **silent** *e* rule are found in words like **changeable** and **peaceable**. In these words the **silent** *e* is kept to make the *g* in **changeable** sound like *j*, and the *c* in **peaceable** sound like *s*.

V. Apply all of the rules you have learned and combine the root words with the suffixes in the space provided below.

1. change + able	
2. venge + ance	
3. oppose + ite	
4. courage + ous	
5. outrage + ous	
6. ridicule + ous	
7. singe + ing	
8. peace + able	
9. fame + ous	
10. notice + able	

VI. Fill in the blanks.

To add the suffix **able** to the root word **notice** we must_____(keep / drop) the **silent e**. The **silent e** is _____(kept / dropped) because of the_____ (**s sound / vowel**) at the _____(**beginning / end**) of the _____(**root word/ suffix**).

More Exceptions to the Rule

There are a few exceptions that have been forced to hang on to the **silent e** regardless of the surrounding influence of other letters. There are also other exceptions that have dropped their **silent e** for no apparent reason. These words must simply be committed to memory for their unique spellings are not associated with any patterns or rules.

VII. Study these exceptions to the rules by writing each word in the space provided below.

1. acknowledge + ment = **acknowledgment**	**acknowledgement** is also acceptable.
2. acre + age = **acreage**	
3. argue + ment = **argument**	
4. awe + ful = **awful**	
5. canoe + ing = **canoeing**	
6. dye + ing = **dyeing**	
7. judge + ment = **judgment**	**judgement** is also acceptable.
8. nine + th = **ninth**	
9. shoe + ing = **shoeing**	
10. toe + ing = **toeing**	
11. true + ly = **truly**	
12. whole + ly = **wholly**	
13. wise + dom = **wisdom**	

Review Test

VIII. Combine the root words with the suffixes in the space provided below.

1. outrage + ous		21. safe + ty	
2. singe + ing		22. confuse + ion	
3. courage + ous		23. ridicule + ous	
4. peace + able		24. definite + ly	
5. venge + ance		25. notice + able	
6. argue + ment		26. fame + ous	
7. change + able		27. acknowledge + ment	
8. awe + ful		28. have + ing	
9. write + ing		29. acre + age	
10. canoe + ing		30. lose + ing	
11. use + ing		31. shoe + ing	
12. dye + ing		32. love + ing	
13. use + ful		33. toe + ing	
14. judge + ment		34. nine + teen	
15. state + ment		35. true + ly	
16. nine + th		36. nine + ty	
17. sincere + ly		37. whole + ly	
18. accurate + ly		38. oppose + ing	
19. save + ing		39. wise + dom	
20. accuse + ing		40. oppose + ite	

You will probably know most of the meanings for the words in this chapter, but write the definitions for those that are new to you. Additional copies of this form may be printed from the CD that came with this workbook.

Word	Most commonly used definition(s):

You will probably know most of the meanings for the words in this chapter, but write the definitions for those that are new to you. Additional copies of this form may be printed from the CD that came with this workbook.

Word	Most commonly used definition(s):

Rewrite your words

New word:		Practice writing the new word:		

Rewrite your words

New word:		Practice writing the new word:	

Rewrite your words

New word:		Practice writing the new word:		

Rewrite your words

New word:		Practice writing the new word:		

Chapter 08
Puzzle #1

Across

2. giving love

6. making accusations

7. brave

9. 19

13. the other side

14. not winning

15. possessing

Down

1. right on target

3. 90

4. the judge gives the

5. paddling a canoe

7. able to change

8. not clear

10. in opposition

11. coloring clothes

12. 9th

Chapter 08
Puzzle #2

Across

2. absurd

6. using your brain wisely

8. The letter was _____ yesterday.

9. entirely

10. measurement in acres

11. sincerely

Down

1. water can pass through

3. I'm _____ my brain.

4. wild, crazy!

5. with sincerity

7. measurement of miles

9. She's _____ a letter.

Similar But Different

The words in this chapter seem the same to many people, but they are very different in meaning and usage. Often they are mistakenly used in place of the correct word - both in speaking and in writing.

In order to function well in the English language, it is extremely important to master the spelling and usage of these words.

1. accept/except
2. adapt/adopt
3. advise/advice
4. affect/effect
5. ally/alley
6. anecdote/antidote
7. allusion/illusion
8. assistance/assistants
9. beggar/bigger
10. bridal/bridle
11. carton/cartoon
12. complement/compliment
13. decent/descent/dissent
14. desert/desert/dessert
15. device/devise
16. diary/dairy
17. discuss/disgust/discus
18. emigrate/immigrate
19. eminent/imminent
20. farther/further/father

21. formerly/formally
22. incidence/incidents
23. metal/medal/meddle/mettle
24. consolation/constellation
25. instant/instance
26. irrelevant/irreverent
27. censor/sensor/censure/censer
28. lead/led/lead
29. liable/libel
30. loose/lose
31. miner/minor
32. moral/morale
33. pedal/peddle/petal
34. persecute/prosecute
35. personal/personnel
36. picture/pitcher
37. precede/proceed
38. presents/presence
39. principal/principle
40. prophesy/prophecy

To become more familiar with each word, we have provided the most common definitions for each word in the exercise below. It would also be advisable that you have a dictionary (and an audio dictionary) at your workspace, to help you in mastering these challenging words.

I. Write each word in a sentence to further develop your understanding of that word:

1. accept – to receive (hint: the two Cs look like outstretched hands)

   _____

   except – all or everyone but … (not that or you) (hint: the x in the word indicates exclusion, or a crossing out)

   _____

2. adapt – to fit in

   _____

   adopt – 1. to take in and care for as one of your own; 2. accept and use

   _____

3. advice – 1. words or knowledge that are designed to help a person. (hint: usually the person, or persons, receiving the advice are using their ears to hear it. The c in advice can remind you of the shape of an ear). 2. The message.

   _____

   advise – to give words or knowledge (hint: often a person who is giving advice is standing. The s in advise can remind you of a person standing, and giving advice)

   _____

4. affect – to move or stir the emotions

   _____

   effect – the result of a cause

   _____

5. ally – a person or nation that is on your side, or strongly favors your position

_____

alley – a corridor between buildings

_____

6. antidote – a remedy for a poison (hint: the prefix anti means against. An antidote is against the poison.)

_____

anecdote – a short, often amusing, story

_____

7. allusion – an reference to something else

_____

illusion – 1. a mistaken idea or impression; 2. making something seem real when it is not

_____

8. assistance - help

_____

assistants - helpers

_____

9. beggar – one who begs

_____

bigger – larger than something, or someone else

_____

129

10. bridal – pertaining to the bride or wedding (hint-Al went to see his bride at the brid<u>al</u> party.)

_____

bridle – 1. a head harness for guiding a horse; 2. to control

_____

11. carton – a container

_____

cartoon – a funny illustration

_____

12. complement – that which completes or brings to perfection

_____

compliment – something said in admiration or praise

_____

13. decent – modest, of good taste

_____

descent – 1. to go downward; 2. one's heritage

_____

dissent – to disagree (hint: the prefix dis means not. To dissent is to <u>not</u> give your approval.)

_____

14. desert – to abandon, leave without permission

_____

dessert – rich tasting food

_____

desert – dry, hot, barren land

_____

15. device – an instrument used for accomplishing a purpose, a tool

_____

devise – to create something, to create a plan

_____

16. dairy – 1. a place where cows are milked; 2. a place where (mainly) milk and milk products are sold

_____

diary – a book in which a person records their most intimate thoughts and experiences

_____

17. discuss – to talk over

_____

disgust – a feeling of strong dislike for someone or something

_____

discus – a heavy circular plate of stone or metal used in tests of strength

_____

18. emigrate – to leave a country

_____

immigrate – to enter another country

_____

19. eminent – well known and respected

_____

imminent – about to happen very soon

_____

20. farther – at a greater distance than the thing being compared (usually physical)

_____

further – more, or in addition to, what has already been stated or shown (usually mental, usually non-physical)

_____

21. formerly – happened in the time already past (hint-from the root former)

_____

formally – to dress very well and dignified for an occasion (hint-from the root formal)

_____

22. incidence – 1. the act of falling upon or influencing; 2. an occurrence; 3. frequency of something that occurs

_____

incidents – 1. occurrences, 2. events; 3. an interruption in the normal flow of things

_____

23. metal– a substance such as gold, tin, lead, copper, etc.

_____

medal – an award pin or insignia

_____

meddle – to interfere

_____

mettle – strength, especially strength of character

_____

24. consolation– the act of giving sympathy (hint: from the word console)

_____

constellation – a group of stars

_____

QUIZ

II. Write the correct answer to each sentence in the space provided.

1. Will you _____(accept/except) that job offer?

2. I'd like to _____ (adapt/adopt) that baby.

3. I would _____(advice/advise) you to study more.

4. What _____ (affect/effect) did the tornado have on your town?

5. She is my closest _____ (alley/ally).

6. Do you have an _____ (anecdote/antidote) for a snake bite?

7. The disappearing elephant trick is just an _____ (allusion/illusion).

8. Have you hired the new dental _____ (assistance/assistants)?

9. My brother is _____ (beggar/bigger) than yours.

10. We went to the _____ (bridle/bridal) shop to buy our wedding dress.

11. I received a _____ (compliment/complement) from my principal for my outstanding grades last semester.

12. We walked down a steep _____ (decent/descent).

13. It's very hot in the _____ (dessert/desert).

14. What kind of _____ (devise/device) is that, and what is it used for?

15. I wrote about my sweetheart in my _____ (dairy/diary).

16. You _____ (disgust/discuss) me!

17. We had to _____ (immigrate/emigrate) from Russia in order to avoid persecution.

18. Did you read the Snoopy _____ (carton/cartoon) in today's paper?

19. We saw the dark clouds, and we knew that a storm was _____ (eminent/imminent).

20. I'd like to discuss that _____ (farther, further) with you.

More Similar but Different Words

25. instant - 1. a particular moment; 2. without delay; 3. a very short space of time

_____

instance – an example, an illustration, occurrence

_____

26. irrelevant – not relevant, not related to

_____

irreverent – without respect, rude

_____

27. censor – 1. (n) One who decides what is appropriate and what is not appropriate; 2. (v) to rule as unacceptable

_____

sensor – a device that receives a signal

_____

censure – to chastise for inappropriate behavior

_____

censer – a container usually filled with a type of incense used in religious ceremonies

_____

28. lead – to direct (present tense)

_____

led – 1. past tense of lead; 2. having directed someone or something.

_____

lead – 1. a bluish gray metal; 2. a heavy weight

_____

29. liable – 1. responsible for; 2. likely to do

libel – A legal proceeding as a result of a false and malicious statement, sign, picture, or effigy tending to expose a person to public ridicule, hatred, contempt, or to damage the person's reputation.

30. loose – 1. to set free; 2. to be free, 3. unchained, unfettered; 4. not tight

lose – to not remember where something is

31. miner – one who digs in the earth for metal, diamonds, gold, etc.

minor – 1. less significant, 2. too young; 3. less in amount

32. moral – 1. good, upright, pure; 2. good message contained in a story

morale – the feeling of worth that a person has

33. pedal – 1. a lever used by the foot; 2. to pedal a bike

peddle – to go from place to place selling small items

petal – the parts or leaves of the corolla of a flower

34. persecute – to harm physically or mentally without provocation

_____

prosecute – to bring legal proceedings against

_____

35. personal – belonging to a person

_____

personnel – referring to those who work for a company

_____

36. picture – a photograph, a painting

_____

pitcher – 1. a container for water; 2. a player on a baseball team who throws balls and strikes

_____

37. precede – to come before (hint – pre means to come before)

_____

proceed – to go forward (hint-pro means to go forward)

_____

38. presents – 1. gifts; 2. to show, give (hint-presen<u>ts</u> and gif<u>ts</u> end in <u>ts</u>)

_____

presence - attendance

_____

39. principal – 1. a person who is the head of a school; 2. money due on a loan after interest monies; 3. main, first, foremost, most important (hint-a principal should be our pal.)

_____

principle – a moral, a standard of conduct; basic truth, law

_____

40. prophesy – (v) to foretell the future. (hint-One who does this is usually standing = s in prophesy)

_____

prophecy – (n) a statement about future events (hint-one who hears a prophecy has ears which are shaped like the letter c in prophecy.)

_____

41. elicit – to draw forth

_____

illicit – not permitted, not allowed by law

_____

Quiz

III. Write the correct answer to each sentence in the space provided.

1. I like _____ (instance/instant) pudding.

2. He was very _____ (irrelevant/irreverent) when the police officer asked him to step out of the car.

3. Why did the committee _____ (censor/censure) that book?

4. She _____ (led/lead) the team in awards this year.

5. I'm not _____ (libel/liable) for your wrong actions.

6. The convict tried to break _____ (lose/loose) from the prison.

7. It was a _____ (minor/miner) violation of the law.

8. This company is a good company, and the workers have good _____ (moral/morale).

9. The _____ (petal/peddle/pedal) fell off my bike.

10. Some people are _____ (prosecuted/persecuted) for their crimes, while others escape.

11. My boss sent me to the _____ (personnel/personal) department to meet the new applicant for the secretarial position.

12. The _____ (pitcher/picture) fell from the wall during the earthquake.

13. Even though Fred is not present, we should _____ (proceed/precede) with the meeting.

14. I hope I get some really nice _____ (presence/presents) for my birthday.

15. The _____ (principle/principal) encouraged us to succeed.

16. Have you read the _____ (prophesy/prophecy) about the battle of Armageddon?

17. You should not _____ (metal/medal/meddle) in other people's business.

18. Will you _____ (accept/except) the blame for your actions?

19. Great Britain was our _____ (ally/alley) in both World Wars.

20. We went to the _____ (diary/dairy) for some milk and cheese.

21. What did you have for _____ (desert/dessert)?

22. The _____ (sensor/censure/censer/censor) detected the intruder and sounded the alarm.

23. What is the _____ (morale/moral) of that story?

24. She was _____ (formally/formerly) known as Sandra Watson, but now she is known as Sandra Jimenez.

25. My _____ (presents/presence) was missed at the school where I once taught, and that made me very happy.

26. The teacher tried to (elicit/illicit) a response from the sleepy class.

You will probably know most of the meanings for the words in this chapter, but write the definitions for those that are new to you. Additional copies of this form may be printed from the CD that came with this workbook.

Word	Most commonly used definition(s):

You will probably know most of the meanings for the words in this chapter, but write the definitions for those that are new to you. Additional copies of this form may be printed from the CD that came with this workbook.

Word	Most commonly used definition(s):

Rewrite your words

New word:		Practice writing the new word:		

Rewrite your words

New word: **Practice writing the new word:**

Rewrite your words

New word:		Practice writing the new word:		

Rewrite your words

New word:		Practice writing the new word:		

Chapter 09
Words: 01-10

Across

1. short amusing story

3. to adjust to

5. how it touches you

6. horse's harness

8. works against a poison

10. indirect reference

12. good to consider

13. helpers

15. narrow passage between buildings

Down

1. to receive

2. to exclude

4. help

5. to take in and care for

7. cause and _____

9. related to wedding

10. to council

11. not reality

14. a friend

Chapter 09
Words: 11-20

Across

2. personal written record

3. at a greater distance

4. round metal object used in Olympics

6. treat after dinner

10. sells milk products

12. to enter a new country

13. distinguished

14. dad

15. of good taste

Down

1. a tool

2. to leave

3. additional

5. praise

7. to leave a country

8. to complete something

9. soon to happen

10. strong dislike

11. to create

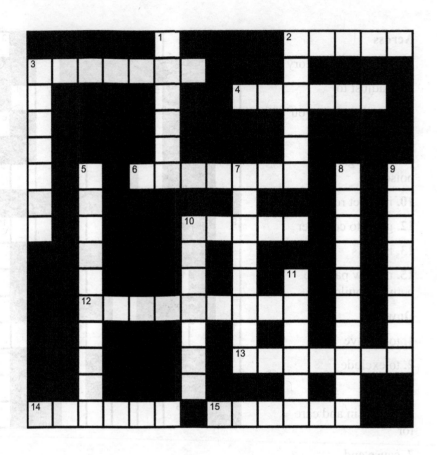

Chapter 09
Words 21-30

Across

1. to interfere

6. picks up a signal

8. guilty of slander

10. legally responsible

12. free

14. iron, cooper, lead, etc

15. holds incense

16. quick

17. not related to the discussion

Down

1. an award badge

2. past tense of lead

3. sympathy

4. character

5. in a dignified manner of dress

7. to rebuke

9. before this time

11. to guide

12. opposite of win

13. an example

15. to control

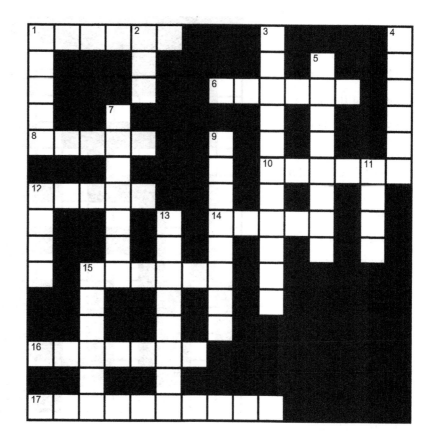

Across

2. just, right, good

5. gifts

6. part of a flower

7. head of the school

9. feelings

10. to try because of a crime

12. photo

13. to give a prophecy

14. to come before

Down

1. being there

2. one who digs in the earth

3. part of a bike

4. given by a prophet

5. throws balls and strikes

7. very close to you

8. to hurt without reason

10. to make a bike go

11. less in amount or significance

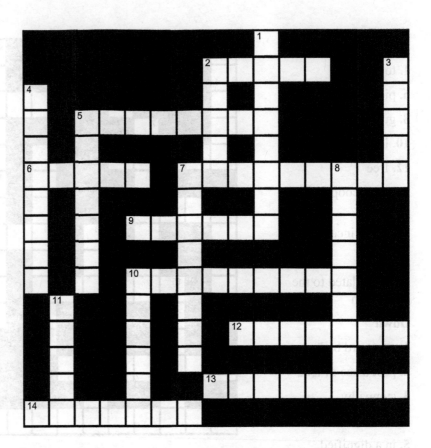

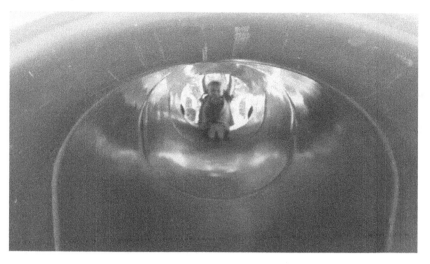

Chapter 10
More Similar but Different Words

As in the previous chapter, the words in this chapter may seem the same to many people, but they are very different in meaning and usage. Often they are mistakenly used in place of the correct word - both in speaking and in writing.

In order to function well in the English language, it is extremely important to master the spelling and usage of these words. The exercises on the following pages will help you to do that.

1. quiet/quite/quit
2. respectfully/respectively
3. shudder/shutter
4. summary/summery
5. then/than
6. obsolete/absolute
7. where/wear/ware/were
8. war/wore
9. viral/virile
10. sink/sync
11. shoo/shoe
12. rational/rationale
13. corpse/corps (ps is silent)/core
14. differ/defer
15. fiber/fibber
16. diner/dinner
17. coma/comma
18. biter/bitter
19. breach/broach
20. tow/toe
21. former/formal

22. costume/custom
23. sleigh/slay
24. whine/wine
25. bite/bit and byte/bit
26. rhythm/rhyme
27. nay/neigh
28. heal/heel
29. position/possession
30. singing/singeing
31. bass/base
32. sewer/sower
33. curser/cursor
34. pour/pore/poor
35. course/coarse
36. horse/hoarse
37. bread/bred
38. Maine/main/mane
39. peel/peal
40. conscience/conscious
41. dose/doze
42. doe/dough

To become more familiar with these words, we have provided the most common definitions for each word in the exercise below. It would also be advisable that you have a dictionary (and an audio dictionary) at your workspace, to help you in mastering these challenging words.

I. Write each word in a sentence to further develop your understanding of that word:

1. quiet – still, silent, calm

    quite – entirely, completely, truly; wholly, to extreme, maximum; actually, really; to a degree, somewhat

    quit – to stop, to end

_____

2. respectfully – with respect or reverence, honor

_____

    respectively – relating to two or more persons or things, one by one, individually

_____

3. shudder – to shake with cold or fear, shiver, vibrate

_____

shutter – 1. movable screen or cover for a window; 2. a device for opening or closing the aperture of a camera.

_____

4. summary – a brief restatement of something read; condense

_____

summery – of, like, or typical of summer

_____

5. then – indicating the next item to follow

_____

than – a comparison between two items

_____

6. obsolete - no longer in use

_____

absolute – without a doubt

_____

7. where - asking the location of something or someone (Where is Josephine?)

_____

wear – 1. to erode; 2. to carry or have on the person (hint-most of what you w<u>ear</u> is below your ears.)

_____

were – past tense of are (We were at home.)

_____

ware – items of the same general type (examples: glassware, dinnerware, hardware, software)

_____

8. wore – 1. past tense of wear; 2. had on as a covering; 3. eroded

_____

war – Armed conflict

_____

9. viral – from a virus

_____

virile – manly, masculine

_____

10. sink – a metal or porcelain tub for washing small items in

_____

sync – to be in harmony; together (synchronize)

_____

11. shoo – to chase away

_____

shoe – a covering worn on the foot

_____

12. rational – reasonable, makes sense

_____

rationale – the underlying reason why something makes sense

_____

13. corpse – a dead body

corps – (the ps is silent) a group

core – the center of something

14. differ – to be different, unlike; opposed to

defer – to put off until later

15. fiber – the coarseness (found in grain and other sources) that helps in digestion

fibber – one who tells (usually harmless) untruths to gain attention

16. diner – 1. one who dines; 2. a place where one dines

dinner – a meal usually eaten in the evening

17. coma – a state of unconsciousness

comma – a punctuation mark indicating a pause when reading

18. biter – one who bites

_____

bitter – sour, not sweet

_____

19. breach – 1. infraction or violation of the law; 2. not to fulfill an obligation

_____

broach – 1. make known for the first time; 2. to open for discussion

_____

20. tow – to pull

_____

toe – a part of the foot

_____

21. former – previous, earlier

_____

formal – in a dignified manner

_____

22. costume – clothing worn to portray a certain image

_____

custom – a particular way of doing something that is, or has been, widely accepted by many persons.

_____

23. sleigh – a buggy on runners used to transport people, or goods, on snow

_____

slay – to kill

_____

24. whine – to complain in a moaning manner

_____

wine – an alcoholic beverage made from grapes or other fruits

_____

25. bite – to clamp the teeth onto or into something

_____

bit – the past tense of bite

_____

26. rhythm – 1. beat of the music; 2. measured flow in poetry

_____

rhyme – words that are sounded alike to create a rhythm

_____

27. nay – no

_____

neigh – sound of a horse

_____

28. heal – to cure

_____

heel – 1. the rear part of the foot; 2. an untrustworthy man; 3. to heel a dog.

_____

29. position – 1. the place where a person, or player, is to stand and play in a game such as baseball, football, tennis, etc; 2. a rank.

_____

possession – 1. to have, to own; 2. to be demonized

_____

30. singing – vocalizing music

_____

singeing – scorching, lightly burning

_____

31. bass – 1. a type of fish; 2. the lowest notes in music

_____

base – 1. foundation; 2. vulgar; 3. a marker used in baseball

_____

32. sewer – 1. a place where trash or refuse flows; 2. one who sews fine clothing

_____

sower – one who sows seeds

_____

33. curser – a person who curses (uses profane words)

cursor – a marker on a computer screen (often flashing and indicating your point of reference on the screen)

34. pour – to empty out

pore – an opening (such as in the skin)

poor – 1. lacking a strong financial position; 2. in a bad, sad or sorry condition

35. course – 1. a path; 2. an area of academic study

coarse – rough, unfinished

36. horse – an animal upon which a person may saddle up and ride

hoarse – rough sounding

37. bread – a food made with yeast, flour, oil, and water as the main ingredients

bred – raised in a certain manner

38. Maine – a state on the East coast of the United States

main – the most important, the primary, the first

mane – the hair on the back of a horse's neck

39. peel – to skin something (such as to peel an apple)

peal – to sound loudly (such as the peal of a bell)

40. conscience – an inner "voice" that suggests right from wrong actions

conscious – alert, awake, aware

41. dose – A measurement, an amount (a dose of medicine)

doze – to fall off into a light sleep

42. doe – a female deer

_____

dough – 1. flour, water, oil, and yeast as the main ingredients combined to make bread; 2. slang for money.

_____

Quiz

I. Write the correct answer to each sentence in the space provided

1. We live on a _____ (quiet/quite) street.

2. I __ _____ (respectively/respectfully) disagree with you.

3. I _____ (shutter/shudder) to think of another season of cold weather.

4. Please analyze the article, don't just give me a brief _____ (summary/summery).

5. He just joined the Marine _____ (corpse/corps/core).

6. I had a _____ (virile/viral) infection and had to stay at home all week.

7. The couple sang a beautiful duet, and the director commented that they were in _____ (sink/sync).

8. My sister plays the _____ (base/bass) guitar.

9. The Senator from New York decided to _____ (defer/differ) his allotted time to the Senator from Connecticut.

10. After the accident, the driver went into a _____ (coma/comma).

11. What _____ (possession/position) do you play on the baseball team?

12. She decided to dress _____ (formally/formerly) for the prom dance.

13. We had a great _____ (diner/dinner) at that _____ (diner/dinner).

14. That discussion sounds _____ (rationale/rational) but can you support it with documentation?

15. The troop _____ (moral/morale) was very good after they heard of the support from their fellow citizens.

16. _____ (fibber/fiber) is good for you digestive system.

17. The judge determined that there was not a _____ (breach/broach) of the law.

18. They decided to _____ (broach/breach) a new subject even though the hour was late.

19. His _____ conscience/conscious began to bother him, so he returned the stolen goods.

20. The _____ costume/custom in that culture is to take good care of the elderly.

21. We visited the Swiss Alps and went for a _____ slay/sleigh ride in the snow.

22. Would you like some cheese with your glass of _____ whine/wine?

23. She took _____ position/possession of the lost dog.

24. The river _____ wear/war/where/wore away the sides of the riverbank - causing the homes along the edge to slip into the water.

25. I can't find the _____ curser/cursor on my computer screen.

You will probably know most of the meanings for the words in this chapter, but write the definitions for those that are new to you. Additional copies of this form may be printed from the CD that came with this workbook.

Word	Most commonly used definition(s):

You will probably know most of the meanings for the words in this chapter, but write the definitions for those that are new to you. Additional copies of this form may be printed from the CD that came with this workbook.

Word	Most commonly used definition(s):

Rewrite your words

New word:		Practice writing the new word:		

Rewrite your words

New word:		Practice writing the new word:	

Rewrite your words

New word:		Practice writing the new word:		

Rewrite your words

New word:		Practice writing the new word:		

Chapter 10
Words 01-10

Across

1. to shiver

4. opposite of peace

5. one by one

6. together

7. no noise

9. items of the same general type

12. entirely

15. condense

17. comparison between two items

18. no longer in use

Down

1. aperture of camera

2. with respect

3. to stop or end

4. what location?

8. next

10. without a doubt

11. summer like

13. to have on as clothes

14. type of infection

15. a tub for washing dishes

16. past tense of are

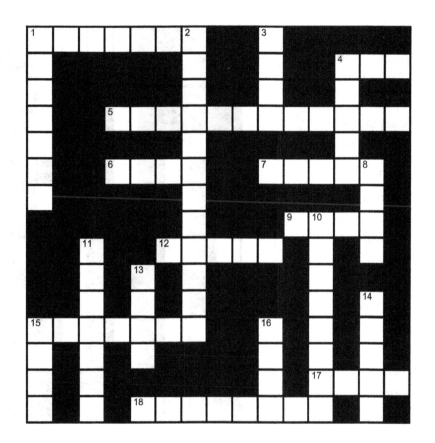

Across

1. teller of "White lies"

4. sour

6. not the same

8. reasonable

9. center

10. unconscious in a
_____

12. dead body

14. one of ten on the foot

15. chase away

16. to bring up, to begin

Down

2. one who bites

3. evening meal

4. to break a promise

5. underlying reasons

6. one who dines

7. coarse material in food that is good for health

10. Marine _____

11. to put off

12. a pause in a sentence

13. wear on your foot

14. to pull

Chapter 10
Words 21-30

Across

2. sound of a horse

5. past tense of bite

6. back of foot

7. particular way of doing something

9. moaning complaint

10. rank

11. Santa's _____

12. earlier

14. make well

15. no

16. scorching

Down

1. the beat

3. alcoholic beverage made from grapes

4. to have

5. to clamp teeth onto

7. clothing worn to portray a certain image

8. vocalizing music

11. to kill

13. to sound alike

Chapter 10
Words 31-42

Across

1. to empty out

2. slang for money

4. type of fish; low notes

6. a person who curses

7. opening in the skin

9. rough material

10. raised in a certain manner

12. a state on the East coast of the USA

14. riding animal

16. a route

17. marker on computer screen

19. measured amount

20. "inner voice"

Down

1. little money

3. rough sounding voice

4. made from dough

5. waste moves through it

8. sound of a bell

9. awake

11. to drift off to sleep

13. foundation

15. one who plants seeds

18. to _____ an apple

19. female deer

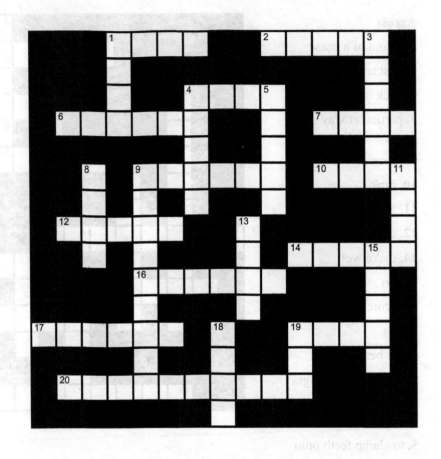

Some Really Confusing Words

Pronunciation, and/or meaning, changes according to context

1. attribute	16. row
2. bass	17. sewer
3. close	18. sow
4. desert	19. subject
5. does	20. tear
6. intimate	21. wind
7. invalid	22. wound
8. lead	23. minute
9. number	24. bureau
10. object	25. cache
11. polish	26. saw
12. present	27. bow
13. produce	28. project
14. read	29. contract
15. refuse	30. articulate

Can you pronounce each word in the list on the previous page? I'm sure that you can pronounce most of them, but oddly enough, each of these words has at least two very different pronunciations. Your pronunciation might be very different from someone else's pronunciation. These words need to be placed in the **context** of a sentence in order for you to know their correct pronunciation

I.   Here are some common meanings for the words in the list above. You may want to refer to your dictionary for a fuller understanding of each word. It is also a good idea to have an audio dictionary handy so that you can clearly hear the different pronunciations of each word. Write a sentence for each word meaning:

1. **attribute** – a certain quality that a person has, talent, physical features

_____

attribute – to give recognition to, to credit with

_____

2. **bass** – a type of fish

_____

bass – a deep sound or tone

_____

3.   **close** - nearby

_____

close – to shut

_____

4. **desert** – to leave an assigned post

_____

desert – a hot and dry place

_____

5. **does** – more than one female deer

_____

does – 3rd person singular present tense of the word do

_____

6. **intimate** – close physically or by relationship (hint – Your mate should be intimate.)

_____

intimate – to suggest; to accuse

_____

7. **invalid** – not valid, not legal

_____

invalid – confined, not able to move freely about

_____

8. **lead** – 1. to show the way, to direct; 2. the main performer

_____

lead - a heavy, soft, malleable, bluish-gray metallic chemical, etc

_____

9. **number** – a state of losing sensory feeling

_____

number - a symbol showing an amount

_____

10. object – to voice disagreement

_____

    object - a material thing, something that can be seen

_____

11. polish – 1. to shine something; 2. material used in shinning something

_____

    Polish – referring to a person from Poland

_____

12. present – 1. a gift; 2. now (as in past, present, future)

_____

    present – to put forth, to show, to introduce

_____

13. produce – to create, to bring forth

_____

    produce - fruits and vegetables, crops

_____

14. read – to view and understand words

_____

    read - the past tense of read

_____

15. refuse – to say no, to decline

refuse - garbage, trash, items not wanted

16. row – 1. to propel a boat, or ship, using oars; 2. in a series, in a line

row – an uproar, a disturbance, fight (rowdy)

17. sewer – someone who sews

sewer - a place for the run off of waste materials

18. sow – to plant seeds

sow – an adult female pig or hog

19. subject – 1. an area of study; 2. legally bound to obey

subject – a person belonging to a kingdom or country

subject – 1. to put under pressure; 2. to force; 3. to enslave

20. tear – to rip

_____

tear – 1. watery substance falling from an eye, 2. the act of producing tears

_____

21. wind – 1. to turn; to twist; 2. to wrap around something

_____

wind - any noticeable movement of air other than a breeze

_____

22. wound – past tense of wind

_____

wound - an injury to the body usually requiring medical attention

_____

23. minute – 1. sixty seconds; 2. a brief period of time

_____

minute - very small, microscopic

_____

24. bureau – a dresser, a chest of drawers; a writing table with drawers

_____

bureau - a department within the government, an agency, an office

_____

25. cache – a hiding place for supplies; supplies of food hidden

_____

cache - a storage area in a computer

_____

176

26. **saw** – Past tense of see

---

saw – a serrated metal tool used to cut wood, metal, and other materials

---

27. **bow** – The front of a boat

---

bow – to bend in a show of respect or honor

---

bow – 1. a looped ribbon used as a decoration; 2. a bow and arrow

---

28. **project** – to show yourself in a certain manner, to give forth a certain image

---

project – something that needs to be done; a chore; a hobby

---

29. **contract** – an agreement

---

contract – 1. to restrict; 2. to close in; 3. to shrink; 4. to come down with a disease

---

30. **articulate** – able to speak in clearly expressed language; powerful speech

---

articulate – able to pronounce words clearly and distinctly

You will probably know most of the meanings for the words in this chapter, but write the definitions for those that are new to you. Additional copies of this form may be printed from the CD that came with this workbook.

Word	Most commonly used definition(s):

You will probably know most of the meanings for the words in this chapter, but write the definitions for those that are new to you. Additional copies of this form may be printed from the CD that came with this workbook.

Word	Most commonly used definition(s):

Rewrite your words

New word:		Practice writing the new word:	

Rewrite your words

New word:		Practice writing the new word:		

Rewrite your words

New word:

New word:		Practice writing the new word:	

Rewrite your words

New word:		Practice writing the new word:		

Chapter 11
Puzzle #1

Across

1. Please _____ that book to me.

3. The _____ blew through town.

7. I'll be there in a _____.

8. It's a _____ drum.

10. I _____ my good looks to my good fortune.

12. The close relationship was very _____.

13. I _____ my watch yesterday.

15. The movie was sad, so I shed a _____.

17. The _____ is collected on Mondays.

19. I _____ a Honda Accord.

20. I hope you don't _____ SARS.

21. The _____ overflowed into the street.

22. It's hot in the _____.

Down

2. How _____ this work?

4. She has the lucky _____.

5. Maria gave me a nice _____.

6. That deed is _____.

8. The _____ of the F.B.I.

9. What _____ are you studying?

10. Her speeches are very _____.

11. He fell off the _____ of the boat.

14. What is that _____?

16. There was a huge _____ at the local bar.

18. Tanya lives _____ to Mark.

19. What crops did you _____ this year?

Chapter 11
Puzzle #2

Across

5. Please _____ the door.

6. The lawyer yelled, "I _____ your Honor."

7. A dresser can be called a _____.

10. There is a _____ in the curtain.

11. Did you read the _____ before signing?

14. _____ is a very heavy metal.

17. Her strongest _____ is her singing voice.

20. The old pig is our finest ____.

21. The soldier suffered a _____.

22. If you _____ the Army, you will be punished.

Down

1. They were _____ to the will of the dictator.

2. I hate to _____ when asked for help.

3. The Novocain made his teeth feel _____.

4. Can you _____ a movie?

5. There was a _____ of weapons in the mountain hideout.

8. If you pronounce your words well, you are considered very _____.

9. My friend's _____ is to build a boat.

12. Do you like to _____ the boat?

13. The _____ was

not able to go outside without help.

15. The deer were all female _____.

16. Do you know how to use a _____ and arrow?

18. I _____ your resume and decided to grant you an interview.

19. Henry likes to go _____ fishing.

20. I cut the wood with my _____.

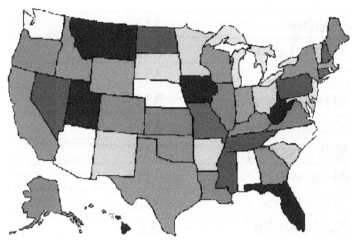

The States of the United States

Many people have not mastered the correct spelling of the States, yet their proper spelling is often required as we go about our daily lives. Recently a team in Illinois was found to have been playing all season with Illinois misspelled as "Illinios" on all of their uniforms. Needless to say it was embarrassing and the team had to wear those uniforms even after the misspelling was noticed because new uniforms were not readily available.

States:	Letter Groupings:	Abbreviations:
1. Alabama	Al/a/bam/a	AL
2. Alaska	A/las/ka	AK
3. Arizona	Ar/i/zon/a	AZ
4. Arkansas	Ar/kan/sas	AR
5. California	Cal/i/for/nia	CA
6. Colorado	Col/or/ado	CO
7. Connecticut	Conn/ec/ti/cut	CT
8. Delaware	Del/a/wa/re	DE
9. Florida	Fl/or/ida	FL
10. Georgia	Geo/r/gia	GA
11. Hawaii	Ha/wa/ii	HI
12. Idaho	Id/a/ho	ID
13. Illinois	Ill/in/ois	IL
14. Indiana	In/dian/a	IN
15. Iowa	Io/wa	IA
16. Kansas	Kan/sas	KS
17. Kentucky	Ken/tuc/ky	KY

States:	Letter Groupings:	Abbreviations:
18. Louisiana	Lou/is/ian/a	LA
19. Maine	Ma/ine	ME
20. Maryland	Mary/land	MD
21. Massachusetts	Mass/a/chu/se/tts	MA
22. Michigan	Mich/i/gan	MI
23. Minnesota	Minn/e/sota	MN
24. Mississippi	Miss/iss/i/pp/i	MS
25. Missouri	Miss/o/uri	MO
26. Montana	Mon/tana	MT
27. Nebraska	Ne/bra/ska	NE
28. Nevada	Ne/va/da	NV
29. New Hampshire	New Hamp/sh/ire	NH
30. New Jersey	New Jer/sey	NJ
31. New Mexico	New Mex/ico	NM
32. New York	New York	NY
33. North Carolina	Nor/th Car/o/lina	NC
34. North Dakota	Nor/th Da/ko/ta	ND
35. Ohio	O/hio	OH
36. Oklahoma	Ok/la/ho/ma	OK
37. Oregon	Ore/gon	OR
38. Pennsylvania	Penn/syl/van/ia	PA
39. Rhode Island	Rh/ode Is/land	RI
40. South Carolina	Sou/th Car/o/lin/a	SC
41. South Dakota	Sou/th Da/ko/ta	SD
42. Tennessee	Tenn/ess/ee	TN
43. Texas	Tex/as	TX
44. Utah	U/tah	UT
45. Vermont	Ver/mont	VT
46. Virginia	Vir/gin/ia	VA
47. Washington	Wash/ing/ton	WA
48. West Virginia	West Vir/gin/ia	WV
49. Wisconsin	Wis/con/sin	WI
50. Wyoming	Wy/o/ming	WY

Rewrite your words

New word:		Practice writing the new word:		

Rewrite your words

New word: **Practice writing the new word:**

New word:		Practice writing the new word:	

I. Rewrite the abbreviation for each state in the box at the right:

States:	Letter Groupings:	Abbreviations:
1. Alabama	Al/a/bam/a	
2. Alaska	A/las/ka	
3. Arizona	Ar/i/zon/a	
4. Arkansas	Ar/kan/sas	
5. California	Cal/i/for/nia	
6. Colorado	Col/or/ado	
7. Connecticut	Conn/ec/ti/cut	
8. Delaware	Del/a/wa/re	
9. Florida	Fl/or/ida	
10. Georgia	Geo/r/gia	
11. Hawaii	Ha/wa/ii	
12. Idaho	Id/a/ho	
13. Illinois	Ill/in/ois	
14. Indiana	In/dian/a	
15. Iowa	Io/wa	
16. Kansas	Kan/sas	
17. Kentucky	Ken/tuc/ky	
18. Louisiana	Lou/is/ian/a	
19. Maine	Ma/ine	
20. Maryland	Mary/land	
21. Massachusetts	Mass/a/chu/se/tts	
22. Michigan	Mich/i/gan	
23. Minnesota	Minn/e/sota	
24. Mississippi	Miss/iss/i/pp/i	
25. Missouri	Miss/o/uri	
26. Montana	Mon/tana	
27. Nebraska	Ne/bra/ska	
28. Nevada	Ne/va/da	
29. New Hampshire	New Hamp/sh/ire	
30. New Jersey	New Jer/sey	
31. New Mexico	New Mex/ico	

32. New York	New York	
33. North Carolina	Nor/th Car/o/lina	
34. North Dakota	Nor/th Da/ko/ta	
35. Ohio	O/hio	
36. Oklahoma	Ok/la/ho/ma	
37. Oregon	Ore/gon	
38. Pennsylvania	Penn/syl/van/ia	
39. Rhode Island	Rh/ode Is/land	
40. South Carolina	Sou/th Car/o/lin/a	
41. South Dakota	Sou/th Da/ko/ta	
42. Tennessee	Tenn/ess/ee	
43. Texas	Tex/as	
44. Utah	U/tah	
45. Vermont	Ver/mont	
46. Virginia	Vir/gin/ia	
47. Washington	Wash/ing/ton	
48. West Virginia	West Vir/gin/ia	
49. Wisconsin	Wis/con/sin	
50. Wyoming	Wy/o/ming	

II. Rewrite the name of each state and its letter grouping in the proper boxes below (use the abbreviation for each state to guide you):

States:	Letter Groupings:	Abbreviations:
1.		AL
2.		AK
3.		AZ
4.		AR
5.		CA
6.		CO
7.		CT
8.		DE
9.		FL
10.		GA
11.		HI
12.		ID
13.		IL
14.		IN
15.		IA
16.		KS
17.		KY
18.		LA
19.		ME
20.		MD
21.		MA
22.		MI
23.		MN
24.		MS
25.		MO
26.		MT
27.		NE
28.		NV
29.		NH
30.		NJ

31.			**NM**
32.			**NY**
33.			**NC**
34.			**ND**
35.			**OH**
36.			**OK**
37.			**OR**
38.			**PA**
39.			**RI**
40.			**SC**
41.			**SD**
42.			**TN**
43.			**TX**
44.			**UT**
45.			**VT**
46.			**VA**
47.			**WA**
48.			**WV**
49.			**WI**
50.			**WY**

Rewrite your words

New word:		Practice writing the new word:		

Rewrite your words

New word:		Practice writing the new word:	

Chapter 12
The States

Across

3. Small State on Chesapeake Bay

5. Horse racing!

7. Corn fields

9. Grand Canyon State

12. Lobsters!

14. Gold Rush; oranges

16. The Everglades

17. Potatoes!

18. Martin Luther King Jr. was born here; sweet peaches

Down

1. Bill Clinton was Governor here.

2. Dorothy and Toto

4. Famous for the Mardi Gras

6. Rocky Mountains

8. Aloha!

10. The Pioneer Space Capital of the World

11. Chicago

13. Indy 500 held here

15. Eskimos and igloos

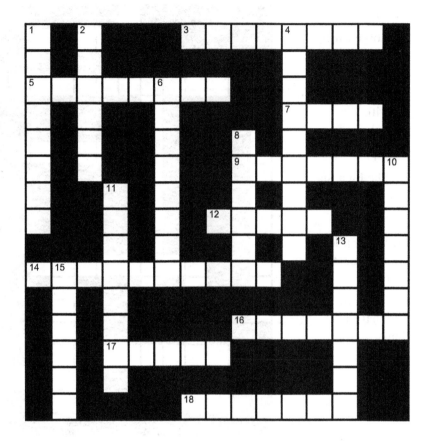

Chapter 12
The States

Across

2. George Bush was Governor here.

5. Boston Marathon; Pilgrims landed here in 1640.

9. The Empire State; Big Apple

10. The First State

11. Famous zoo in Cincinnati

13. Motor town or Motown USA in Detroit

14. Home of the National Bison Range

15. The "Show Me State"

16. Homes made of Adobe bricks

17. Seemingly endless plains

18. Las Vegas

Down

1. Salt Lake City

3. "The Garden State"

4. "The Rice State"

5. Named after our largest river

6. Borders New York on its Western side

7. The Wright Brothers made first airplane flight from Kitty Hawk in 1903.

8. A wind speed of 231 MPH recorded on MT Washington in 1934.

12. Over three million cows graze here.

Chapter 12
The States

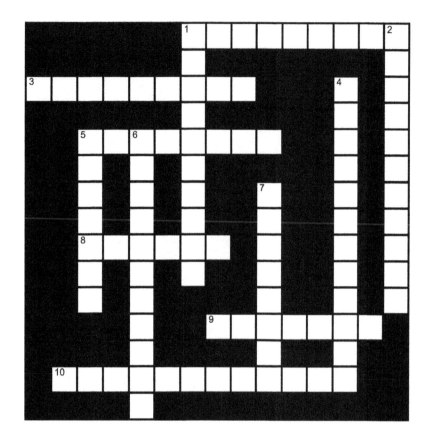

Across

1. Dairy State

3. Grand Ole Opry in Nashville

5. Arlington Cemetery honors War heroes

8. Crater Lake Park

9. Yellowstone Park is home of over 200 geysers.

10. The Declaration of Independence and the Constitution were signed in Philadelphia

Down

1. Mt. St. Helens' volcano erupted here in 1989.

2. The "Badlands" are here

4. Leading USA coal producing State.

5. Famous for Maple Syrup

6. The smallest state

7. The Horse Show Capital of the world

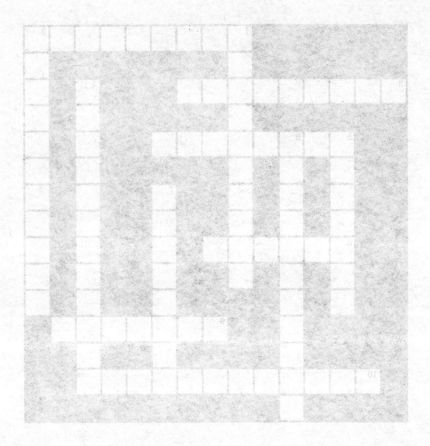

Across

1. Dairy State

3. Grand Ole Opry in Nashville

5. Arlington Cemetery honors War heroes

8. Crater Lake Park

9. Yellowstone Park is home of over 200 geysers.

10. The Declaration of Independence and the Constitution were signed in Philadelphia

Down

1. Mt. St. Helens volcano erupted here in 1980

2. The "Badlands" are here

4. Leading USA coal producing State

5. Famous for Maple Syrup

6. The smallest state

7. The Horse Show Capital of the world

The Use of the Apostrophe "'"'"'"'

The apostrophe (') has several uses. The first, and most common, use of the apostrophe is to show possession. An example might be: *It is Samuel's new Honda.* That sentence shows that the Honda belongs to Samuel – it is his possession.

A second use of the apostrophe is to replace omitted letters or numbers. Can not becomes can't. The apostrophe shows that a contraction has been formed. A contraction is a word that is formed by combining two words and omitting certain letters from them. The apostrophe shows us where, in the word combination, the letters have been omitted.

Numbers can also be shortened. *She was a nurse in the Iraqi war in '03.* The numbers 20 have been omitted from the year 2003.

A third use for the apostrophe is to make plurals of letters or numbers. *Five students received A's on the quiz. Ten 10's equals one hundred.*

Possessive Case

Rule #1: Singular words form the possessive case by adding an ' and an **s**. Let's practice that rule now.

1. It is Jason _____ book.

2. The tornado _____ destruction was widespread over the South.

3. The baseball team ___ winning hit came in the ninth inning.

4. Emilio _____ lunch was left in Maria _____ car.

5. Jay Leno _____ favorite automobile is his 1959 Corvette.

6. The politician ___ bad conduct lost him many votes.

7. Are those Ron _____ tools?

8. Marcie _____ lawnmower is red and black.

9. The salesperson _____ commission can vary from paycheck to paycheck .

10. Jennifer ___ trout won the fishing contest and it weighed eight pounds.

Rule #2: When adding a 's results in an awkward s or z sound, only the apostrophe is used. *Luis' Suburban is the coolest truck in our neighborhood* However please note that *s*ome words like James or Charles would be written as James's or Charles's in the possessive because they present no pronunciation challenge. Let's practice this rule.

1. That is said to be Xerxes _____ sword.

2. Moses _____ request to the Pharaoh was to let his people leave Egypt.

3. The Euphrates _____ currents are very swift.

4. It was Jesus ___ first miracle.

5. Lois ___ dress was beautiful and adorned with diamonds.

Rule #3: Plural words that end in **s** are made possessive by adding only an apostrophe. Let's practice some now.

1. The three cats ___ sweaters were finally finished.

2. Certain spectators _____ behavior was considered rude.

3. Several attorneys _____ cases were thrown out of court.

4. The Lawyers ____ portfolios were designed to prove their case.

5. The players ____ contracts were full of perks.

Rule #4: Irregular plural words that do not end in an **s** are made plural by adding **'s**. *The media's responsibility is to report the news honestly.*

Rule #5: Compound nouns form the possessive by adding either **'s** or just the **'** to the compound part closest to the thing possessed (depending on whether it is singular or plural). *I borrowed my brother-in-law's motorcycle.* or *The two vice presidents' automobiles were made by Mercedes Benz.* Let's practice now.

1. My sister-in-law ___ home is beautiful.

2. Sam and Audrey ___ children are well behaved.

3. King Henry VIII ___ many wives suffered as a result of his evil treatment.

4. That is John D. Rockefeller _____ yacht.

5. The associate professor ___ exams were very difficult.

6. My DVD contains several executive director ___ cuts as a bonus.

Rule #6: When there is separate ownership of an item, both nouns take the possessive case. *The FDA's and FBI's studies arrived at different conclusions.* Let's practice now.

1. Larry ___ and Christy ___ views on childcare are in agreement.

2. Wal-Mart ___ and Kmart ___ profits have risen.

3. Harvard ___ and Yale ___ graduates usually find well paying employment opportunities.

4. George ___ and Samantha ___ wish was to have another child.

5. Iran ___ and Iraq ___ people want freedom from oppression.

Rule #7: The rules that we have studied so far also apply to indefinite pronouns. *Nobody's idea was accepted and all had to think of new ideas.*

1. Someone ___ jacket is lying on the floor.

2. Everyone ___ foolish statements haunt them.

3. No one ___ budget ever seems to have enough cash.

4. One ___ reputation is an important asset is kept clean.

5. Another ___ opinion should at least be considered before making an important decision.

Apostrophe for Missing Letters or Numbers

Rule # 8: An apostrophe is used to show missing letters or numbers. *We can't go to the movies tonight. In '91, we signed a treaty with North Korea to limit nuclear weapons.* The chart below contains the original words and the most common contractions.

1. I am	1. I'm
2. do not	2. don't
3. you are	3. you're
4. did not	4. didn't
5. will not	5. won't
6. I have	6. I've
7. it is	7. it's
8. does not	8. doesn't
9. is not	9. isn't
10. we are	10. we're
11. can not	11. can't

Let's practice now. Write the correct form of the word or number for each example.

1. Jose _____ (does not) live here anymore.

2. _____ (it is) a great price for a new car.

3. I was drafted to fight in Vietnam in _____ (1972).

4. You _____ (can not) park a pickup truck in that small space.

5. _____ (you are) my best friend.

6. _____ (we are) going to a football game on Friday.

7. She _____ (will not) lie.

8. A new strain of the SARS virus is _____ (slang for going) around

.

9. The farmer was _____ (slang for rushing) to harvest the corn before the storm arrived.

10. _____ (do not) cheat your way through school.

Apostrophe for Plural Forms

Rule #9: Most numbers, letters, and abbreviations are made into the plural form by adding **'s**. Some *exceptions* to that rule exist in the case of years that are written out (1998s for example), other long numbers, numbers written as words, and abbreviations without periods. Let's practice.

1. My mother used to say that everyone should mind their p ___ and q__ which meant we should not meddle in another's life.

2. Most of the class scored in the 80 ___ on the quiz.

3. The 1960 ____ was a time of great change.

4. Sandra has earned two Ph.D. ___.

5. There was a convention of M.D. ____ being held at the Civic Center.

I. Add apostrophes to the following sentences unless one is not needed:

1. Joshua ____ friend broke his arm playing baseball.

2. Nathan was born in the 1970___.

3. The farmer ___ field produced some great corn.

4. It ___ anybody ___ guess how far that homerun ball traveled.

5. The boy ___ locker room was a mess.

6. Steinbeck __ novels are very well written.

7. _____ (is not) it time you drove a better car?

8. Your goal should be to earn as many A ___ as possible.

9. _____ (nobody is) watching the children.

10. The Rodriguez _____ family went on a long vacation.

11. The Eagle ___ nest was empty.

12. _____ (I am) not at my best in the morning.

13. Alice said, " _____ (I have) only three semesters left before I graduate."

14. Everybody ___ talking about the upcoming prom.

15. The Children ___ choir sounded very professional.

16. Some say you should never heat the baby ___ bottle in a microwave.

17. Dennis plans to graduate in _____ (2007).

18. Nadia and I ate lunch at Greco ___ deli.

19. Do you have trouble reading 5 ___ and S ___ ?

20. The Joneses _____ children are misbehaving again.

II. Rule Check

Fill in the blanks below to correctly complete each rule:

1. **Rule #1:** Singular words form the possessive case by adding an ____ and an ____.

2. **Rule #2:** When adding a 's results in an awkward s or z sound, only the _____ is used.

3. **Rule #3:** Plural words that end in _____ are made possessive by adding only an apostrophe.

4. **Rule #4:** Irregular plural words that do not end in an _____ are made plural by adding **'s.**

5. **Rule #5:** Compound nouns form the possessive by adding either **'s** or just the **'** to the compound part _____ to the thing possessed (depending on whether it is singular or plural).

6. **Rule #6:** When there is separate ownership of an item, _____ nouns take the possessive case.

7. **Rule #7:** The rules that we have studied so far also apply to indefinite _____.

8. **Rule # 8:** An _____ is used to show missing letters or numbers.

9. **Rule #9:** Most numbers, letters, and abbreviations are made into the plural form by adding _____. Some *exceptions* to that rule exist in the case of _____ that are written out, other long _____, numbers written as _____, and abbreviations without _____.

208

You will probably know most of the meanings for the words in this chapter, but write the definitions for those that are new to you. Additional copies of this form may be printed from the CD that came with this workbook.

Word	Most commonly used definition(s):

Rewrite your words

New word:		Practice writing the new word:		

Chapter 13
Puzzle #1

When working on this puzzle, be sure to leave a space between the two words that correspond to the contraction clue.

Across

1. I'm

4. I've

5. didn't

8. won't

9. you're

Down

1. it's

2. doesn't

3. don't

6. isn't

7. can't

8. we're

Chapter 13
Puzzle #2

When working this puzzle, be sure to put an apostrophe ' in the proper square. When working the puzzle in the web edition, leave a blank where the apostrophe belongs.

Across

1. I am

2. do not

3. you are

4. did not

6. will not

8. I have

Down

1. it is

2. does not

5. is not

6. we are

7. can not

Chapter 14

Challenging Words

The following words have been known to challenge even the best of spellers. They are, however commonly used in the English language.

There are several ways to approach learning these words. You need to determine the best approach for you.

Study cards are available, on the CD Rom included with this workbook, and may be printed out (using MSWord) on paper or card stock. They are designed to print onto business card stock of 10 cards per page. That card stock is readily available at Wal-Mart, Kmart, Staples, Best Buy, and similar stores.

A second approach would be to write each word several times on the enclosed chapter "Rewrite" sheets. (Additional sheets may be printed from your enclosed CD Rom.)

A third approach is to write the word and its definition on the enclosed chapter "Word/Definition" sheet. (Additional sheets may be printed from your enclosed CD Rom.)

The approach that you use will depend on your learning style and your instructor's guidance. It is usually best to learn 10 to 20 words at a time. We have structured the tables to help you to do that.

1. absence (ab/sen/ce)	11. ancestor (an/ces/tor)
2. academic (a/ca/dem/ic)	12. Antarctic (Ant/arc/tic)
3. accidental (acc/i/den/tal)	13. anxiety (anx/ie/ty)
4. accommodate (a/cc/o/mm/o/date)	14. anxious (anx/ious)
5. accuse (a/cc/use)	15. apparently (app/ar/ent/ly)
6. ache (ache)	16. argument (ar/gu/ment)
7. acquainted (ac/qu/ain/ted)	17. awful (aw/ful)
8. acquire (ac/qu/ire)	18. beautiful (beau/ti/ful)
9. advertiser (ad/ver/tis/er)	19. business (bus/i/ness)
10. Arctic (Arc/tic)	20. calendar (cal/en/dar)

21. censor (cen/sor)	31. costume (cos/tume)
22. censure (cen/sure)	32. criticism (cri/ti/cism)
23. citizen (cit/i/zen)	33. decision (de/cis/ion)
24. coincidence (co/in/ci/den/ce)	34. democracy (dem/o/cr/acy)
25. coincidental (co/in/ci/den/tal)	35. ecstasy (ecs/tasy)
26. compliment (com/pli/ment)	36. embarrass (em/barr/ass)
27. congratulate (con/grat/u/late)	37. envelop (en/ve/lop)
28. consumer (con/sum/er)	38. envelope (en/ve/lope)
29. controversial (con/tro/ver/sial)	39. environment (en/vi/ron/ment)
30. convenience (con/ven/ience)	40. equipment (e/quip/ment)

41. especially (es/pe/cia/lly)	51. holiday (hol/i/day)
42. etc. (etc.)	52. hypocrisy (hy/po/crisy)
43. exaggerate (ex/a/gg/er/ate)	53. ignorance (ig/nor/ance)
44. February (Feb/ru/ary)	54. invasion (in/vas/ion)
45. forty (for/ty)	55. irrelevant (irr/el/e/vant)
46. government (gov/ern/ment)	56. island (is/land)
47. governor (gov/er/nor)	57. jealous (jeal/ous)
48. grievous (gr/ie/vous)	58. laboratory (la/bor/a/tory)
49. grocery (gro/cery)	59. language (lang/u/age)
50. height (hei/ght)	60. leather (lea/ther)

You will probably know most of the meanings for the words in this chapter, but write the definitions for those that are new to you. Additional copies of this form may be printed from the CD that came with this workbook.

Word	Most commonly used definition(s):

You will probably know most of the meanings for the words in this chapter, but write the definitions for those that are new to you. Additional copies of this form may be printed from the CD that came with this workbook.

Word	Most commonly used definition(s):

Rewrite your words

New word:	Practice writing the new word:		

Rewrite your words

New word:		Practice writing the new word:		

Chapter 14
Words 01-20

Across

1. extremely disagreeable

3. the state or time of being absent

6. abnormal apprehension and fear often accompanied by psychological signs

7. to charge with an offense, blame

10. an arrangement of time into days, weeks, months and years

11. to gain possession of

12. relating to, or associated with schools or colleges

Down

1. relating to the north pole or the region near it

2. to suffer a dull persistent pain

4. personal knowledge of someone

5. one from whom an individual is descended

6. it seems apparent

7. to call public attention to

8. relating to the south pole or the region near it

9. discourse intended to persuade

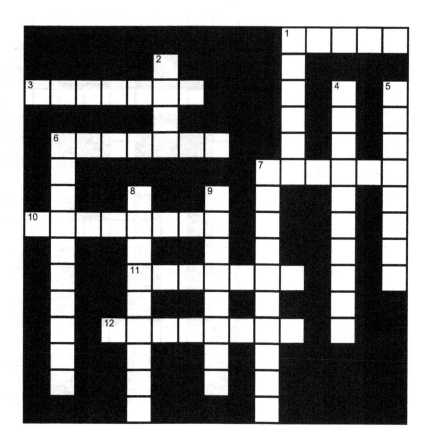

219

Chapter 14
Words 21-40

Across

1. happening at the same time

6. tools

8. government by the people

9. personal comfort

11. use to mail a letter

12. praise someone

Down

2. offer praise

3. intense happiness

4. that which surrounds you

5. Worn on Halloween

6. to humiliate someone

7. an inhabitant of a country

8. when you decide, you come to a ____

10. to surround

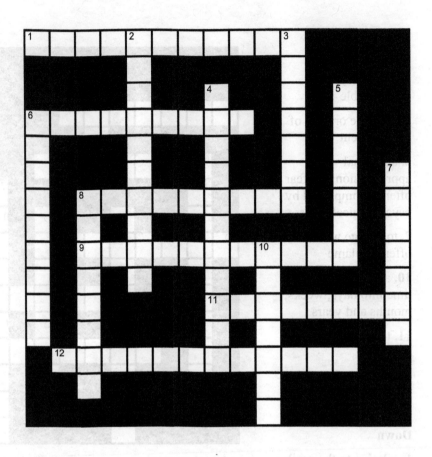

Chapter 14
Words 41-60

Across

1. the false assumption of an appearance of virtue or religion

4. sad situation

5. animal skin dressed for use

7. Christmas, Easter, etc..

10. what a person speaks

11. making more out of something than it really is

12. entry of an army into a country for conquest

13. authoritative direction or control, rule

Down

2. a body of land surrounded by water

3. a number one greater than 39

4. a dealer in staple foodstuff

6. demanding complete devotion

8. not relevant

9. a ruler, chief executive, or head of a political unit

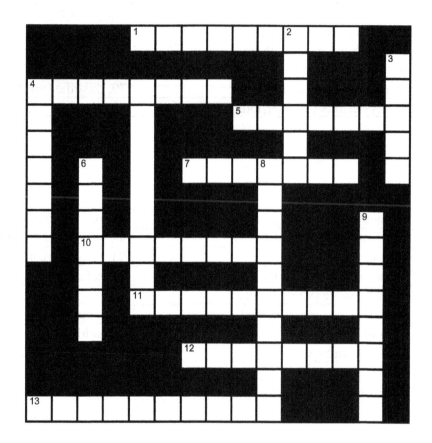

61. length (len/gth)	71. nuclear (nu/cl/ear) or (nu/clear)
62. library (li/br/ary)	72. nuisance (nui/san/ce)
63. license (li/cen/se)	73. oblige (ob/lige)
64. listen (lis/ten)	74. obstacle (ob/sta/cle)
65. maneuver (man/eu/ver)	75. occasion (occ/as/ion)
66. marriage (marr/ia/ge)	76. optimism (op/ti/mism)
67. mischievous (mis/chie/vous)	77. pamphlet (pam/ph/let)
68. mountain (moun/tain)	78. parallel (par/all/el)
69. municipal (mun/i/ci/pal)	79. pastime (pas/time)
70. mysterious (mys/ter/ious)	80. physical (phy/si/cal)

81. picnicking (pic/nic/king)	91. recommend (re/co/mm/end)
82. pleasant (plea/sant)	92. sandwich (sand/wich)
83. poison (poi/son)	93. sausage (saus/age)
84. possession (poss/ess/ion)	94. schedule (sch/ed/ule)
85. vengeance (ven/ge/an/ce)	95. scissors (sci/ss/ors)
86. prejudiced (pre/ju/diced)	96. sergeant (ser/gea/nt)
87. proceed (pro/ceed)	97. soldier (sold/ier)
88. procedure (pro/ced/ure)	98. solemn (sol/emn)
89. pursue (pur/sue)	99. souvenir (sou/ven/ir)
90. recognize (re/cog/nize)	100. spectacular (spec/ta/cu/lar)

101. spectator (spec/ta/tor)	111. temperature (temp/er/a/ture)
102. sponsor (spon/sor)	112. theory (th/eo/ry)
103. strength (st/ren/gth)	113. tolerant (to/ler/ant)
104. stretch (st/re/tch)	114. truly (tru/ly)
105. stubborn (st/u/bb/orn)	115. undoubtedly (un/dou/bt/ed/ly)
106. subtle (sub/tle)	116. villain (vi/ll/ain)
107. succeed (su/cc/eed)	117. warehouse (ware/house)
108. surprise (sur/pri/se)	118. wariness(war/i/ness)
109. technique (tech/ni/que)	119. warranty (wa/rr/an/ty)
110. temperament (temp/er/a/ment)	120. Wednesday (Wed/nes/day)

You will probably know most of the meanings for the words in this chapter, but write the definitions for those that are new to you. Additional copies of this form may be printed from the CD that came with this workbook.

Word	Most commonly used definition(s):

You will probably know most of the meanings for the words in this chapter, but write the definitions for those that are new to you. Additional copies of this form may be printed from the CD that came with this workbook.

Word	Most commonly used definition(s):

Rewrite your words

New word:		Practice writing the new word:		

Rewrite your words

New word:		Practice writing the new word:		

Chapter 14
Words 61-80

Across

1. compare, to correspond to

3. a measured distance

5. irresponsibly playful

7. restricted to one locality

8. a procedure involving expert physical movement

10. an unbound printed publication

11. a place where you get books on loan for a number of days

12. a document, plate, or tag

13. a weapon whose destructive power results from an uncontrolled nuclear reaction

Down

1. diversion, something that makes time pass agreeably

2. relating to the body

4. an annoying or troublesome person or thing

6. expecting a good outcome

7. a landmass higher that a hill

9. to do a favor for

Chapter 14
Words 81-100

Across

1. to go in an orderly way

2. to injure or kill with a chemical

4. something serving as a reminder

6. two pieces of bread with meat or cheese in between

8. punishment inflicted in retaliation for an injury or offense

9. minced and highly seasoned meat (pork) enclosed in tubular casing

10. something owned

11. nice to be around

Down

1. judged without sufficient evidence

2. go after

3. one who fights in a war

4. an officer in a police force

5. to go on a picnic

7. cutting instruments like shears but smaller

Chapter 14
Words 101-120

Across

1. to obtain a desired object or end

3. shrewd, perceptive, clever

5. one who observes

10. to make longer or wider

11. mode of emotional response

12. in a proper or suitable manner

13. a general principle offered to explain items observed

Down

1. one who promotes a product

2. toughness, solidity

4. the manner in which technical details are treated, or basic physical movements are produced

6. degree of hot or cold

7. a written guarantee of the integrity of a product and the repair, or replacement, of parts

8. the body's ability to become less responsive over time to something

9. unexpected

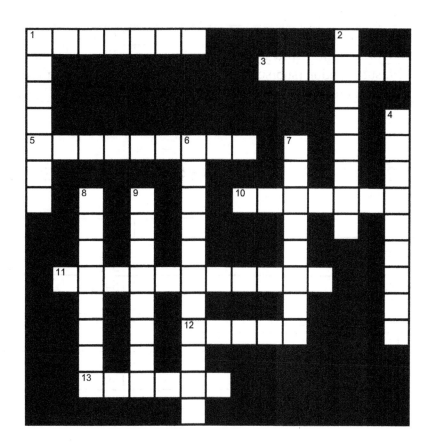

121. comfortable (com/for/table)	131. controversy (con/tro/ver/sy)
122. anguish (ang/ui/sh)	132. controversial (con/tro/ver/sial)
123. magnificent (mag/ni/fi/cent)	133. interior (in/ter/ior)
124. dictionary (dic/tion/ary)	134. exterior (ex/ter/ior)
125. guarantee (guar/an/tee)	135. analysis (an/aly/sis)
126. prescribe (pre/scribe)	136. island (is/land)
127. subscribe (sub/scribe)	137. isle (is/le)
128. prescription (pre/scr/ip/tion)	138. inquire (in/qui/re)
129. subscription (sub/scr/ip/tion)	139. conquer (con/quer)
130. congratulations (con/grat/u/la/tions)	140. misspell (miss/pell) or (mis/spell)

Add your own challenging words in the boxes below:

141.	151.
142.	152.
143.	153.
144.	154.
145.	155.
146.	156.
147.	157.
148.	158.
149.	159.
150.	160.

161.	171.
162.	172.
163.	173.
164.	174.
165.	175.
166.	176.
167.	177.
168.	178.
169.	179.
170.	180.

You will probably know most of the meanings for the words in this chapter, but write the definitions for those that are new to you. Additional copies of this form may be printed from the CD that came with this workbook.

Word	Most commonly used definition(s):

You will probably know most of the meanings for the words in this chapter, but write the definitions for those that are new to you. Additional copies of this form may be printed from the CD that came with this workbook.

Word	Most commonly used definition(s):

Rewrite your words

New word:		Practice writing the new word:		

Rewrite your words

New word:		Practice writing the new word:	

Chapter 14
Words 121-140

Across

1. to spell incorrectly

5. to give security to

6. a written direction for the use of medicine

8. a purchase by signed order

9. a small island

10. to gain by force of arms, win

11. outside surface

Down

2. to write an order for medicine

3. a body of land surrounded by water

4. disputable

7. inside surface

8. to order a magazine

9. to ask about

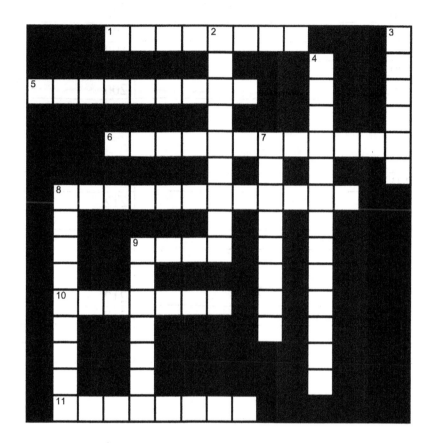

181.	191.
182.	192.
183.	193.
184.	194.
185.	195.
186.	196.
187.	197.
188.	198.
189.	199.
190.	200.

201.	211.
202.	212.
203.	213.
204.	214.
205.	215.
206.	216.
207.	217.
208.	218.
209.	219.
210.	220.

221.	231.
222.	232.
223.	233.
224.	234.
225.	235.
226.	236.
227.	237.
228.	238.
229.	239.
230.	240.

You will probably know most of the meanings for the words in this chapter, but write the definitions for those that are new to you. Additional copies of this form may be printed from the CD that came with this workbook.

Word	Most commonly used definition(s):

You will probably know most of the meanings for the words in this chapter, but write the definitions for those that are new to you. Additional copies of this form may be printed from the CD that came with this workbook.

Word	Most commonly used definition(s):

Rewrite your words

New word:		Practice writing the new word:		

Rewrite your words

New word: **Practice writing the new word:**

New word:			

Common
Prefixes, Roots,
& Suffixes

Learning the commonly used word parts known as prefixes (parts added to the beginning of a word or root), roots (the main part of a word), and suffixes (parts added to the end of a word or root) can help you to figure out, spell, and learn many words even when a dictionary (or friend) is not readily available.

Write the meaning for each word below. It is best to learn five or ten words a day along with the meaning of the appropriate word part. It will help you to make connections with other unfamiliar words that are built around the same word parts.

1. a, an = not, without

amoral	Not moral, without morals
anarchy	Without government
anemia	Without proper oxygen-carrying material in the blood
atheist	One who does not believe in God
atypical	Not typical

2. ambi, amphi – around, both

1. ambiguous	Having a double meaning
2. amphitheater	A theater that surrounds the audience
3. ambidextrous	Able to use both hands equally
4. ambiguity	Having a double or unclear meaning
5. amphibian	Able to live both on land and water

3. ann, enn –year, yearly

1. annals	Accounts of yearly activity arranged in sequence
2. anniversary	Yearly celebration of an event
3. annual	Occurring yearly
4. annuity	A yearly payment
5. millennium	A thousand years

4. ante -before

1. antedate	To date before
2. anteroom	A room that comes before the main room
3. antebellum	Before the U. S. Civil War
4. antecedent	One who, or that which, goes before in time
5. antemeridian	Before noon

5. ant, anti = against

antagonist	one who works against another
antibiotic	works against the life of a disease causing agent
antidote	remedy for a poison
antiseptic	works against septic items
Antarctica	Against the Arctic (South vs. North Pole)

6. anthrop - human

1. anthropologist	One who studies ancient human remains &cultures
2. anthropology	The study of ancient human remains & cultures
3. misanthrope	A person who does not fit in well with society
4. philanthropist	One who gives generously to humanity
5. philanthropy	Love towards mankind

7. itis – inflammation of

1. appendicitis	Inflammation of the appendix
2. bronchitis	Inflammation of the air passages within the lungs
3. iritis	Inflammation of the iris of the eye
4. arthritis	Inflammation of the joints of the fingers or toes
5. vasculitis	Inflammation of the blood vessels

8. auto-self

1. automatic	Runs by itself
2. automobile	Moves by itself (under its own power)
3. autonomous	Self governing
4. autonomy	The right of self government
5. autopsy	Seeing for yourself the cause of death

9. bene - well, good

1. benefactor	One who gives generously
2. beneficial	Good for you or others
3. beneficiary	One who receives good benefits
4. benefit	A good thing
5. benevolent	Having good characteristics

10. bi = two

bicycle	a cycle with two wheels
bigamy	being married to two persons at the same time
bilingual	able to speak two languages
binoculars	two lens able to see at a great distance
bipartisan	able to work with both parties

11. bio = life

autobiography	a life story written by oneself
biodegradable	able to degrade (breakdown) the life
biography	a story written about a life
biology	study of life
biopsy	a looking at the life of a tissue

12. chron, chrono = time

chronic	occurring over time
chronicle	a written account of a time period
chronology	a logical time order
chronometer	a device used to measure time
synchronize	to set time pieces to the same time

13. circum-around

1. circumference	The outer surface of a round object
2. circumscribe	To draw a line around; create a boundary
3. circumspect	Watchful on all sides; examining all sides
4. circumstance	Standing around an event
5. circumvent	Getting around something through deception

14. co- together, with

1. coherent	Making sense; being together in speech
2. coincide	To happen at the same point in time
3. coincident	Happening at the same time
4. coherence	Easily understood because it is organized together
5. cooperate	To work well together

15. col- together, with

1. collaborate	To work together on something
2. collusion	To conspire together
3. collide	To come together forcefully
4. collage	To put together pieces to make a whole artfully
5. collapse	To fall together

16. com- together, with

1. commend	Bringing together praise
2. committee	Group of people who come together to work on a project
3. commotion	With movement or agitation
4. companion	One who associates with another on a regular basis
5. complicate	With complexity

17. con- together, with

1. condominium	Joint rule or control
2. condone	Agree with
3. conception	Bringing together an idea or life
4. congenital	Being with a person from birth
5. contemporary	Being with the temporary (or current) things

18. cred-to believe

1. credentials	Papers that prove the truth of something
2. credible	Able to believe
3. credit	Money loaned based on the belief that it will be paid back
4. discredit	To state (or prove) a disbelief in someone or something
5. incredible	1. Not able to believe. 2. Almost beyond belief.

19. cor - together, with

1. correlate	Having a relationship with
2. corporate	Belonging to the body of a large business
3. corporation	A large business that had combined smaller ones
4. corps	A group of persons working together (troops)
5. correspond	To reply with another

20. dem - people

1. demagogue	A person who sways the people by oratory
2. democracy	Government of the people
3. endemic	Peculiar to a certain group of persons
4. epidemic	Spreading through the population
5. pandemic	Spreading through the population

21. di – not, away, apart

1. diverse	Many parts
2. diversion	A turning away from the usual
3. divide	Breaking apart
4. divorce	Dividing into two parts
5. divulge	Giving away information

22. dict - to speak

1. addict	Speaking to
2. contradict	Speaking against
3. dictate	to speak out
4. dictionary	to speak the meanings of words
5. predict	To speak beforehand of future events

23. dis – not, away, apart

1. disarray	Not in order
2. disaster	Not good according to the stars
3. disconcert	Not in order (concert), throw into confusion
4. discordant	Not in agreement (not in accord)
5. disease	Not at ease; not healthy

24. e - out

1. educate	To draw knowledge out; to give knowledge out
2. erupt	To throw out
3. eject	To toss out
4. emit	To give out
5. eradicate	To erase out

25. ex - out

1. excavate	To bring out
2. exclaim	To call out
3. exodus	To go out from a place or country
4. expel	To toss out
5. exit	To go out

26. fid - faith

1. bona fide	true
2. confidant	One you can truly share your thoughts with
3. confide	To have faith to share with
4. confidential	Shared with faith that it will be kept private
5. fidelity	Faithful to promise

27. gen - birth, race, kind

1. generate	To create or birth
2. generation	Common period of time shared by persons
3. genesis	The beginning
4. genius	Original thinker; originator of ideas
5. ingenious	Well conceived (birthed)

28. graph – to write, writing, drawing

1. autograph	Written by oneself
2. calligraphy	The art of beautiful writing
3. choreography	The art of designing & arranging dance
4. geography	Drawings or writings of the earth
5. graphic	Clearly written

29. gram - to write, writing, drawing

1. cardiogram	Writings of the heart rhythms
2. diagram	A drawing describing the parts of something
3. epigram	A short (usually satirical) poem
4. telegram	Writing sent across a distance
5. monogram	One written (or embroidered) letter

30. log - speech, word

1. analogous	Bearing some resemblance despite differences
2. analogy	A likeness between things
3. apology	Something said in defense or regret
4. dialogue	Words between two or more persons
5. monologue	One person speaking

31. logy-study of

1. archeology	Study of remains of earlier cultures
2. psychology	Study of the psyche (mind)
3. ecology	Study of the environment
4. embryology	Study of embryos
5. biology	Study of life

32. mal-bad

1. malady	Disease, disorder
2. malaise	State of being ill
3. malaria	Disease caused by mosquitoes (literally means bad air)
4. malice	Ill will towards others
5. malign	Badly aligned

33. meter, metr-measure

1. barometer	Measure of air pressure
2. kilometer	1000 meters
3. thermometer	Instrument used to measure temperature
4. tachometer	Instrument used to measure velocity
5. metronome	Measures (beats) time for musicians

34. mono-one

1. monogamy	Married to one person
2. monocle	Eyepiece for one eye only
3. monolith	A pillar formed of a single stone
4. monopoly	An exclusive trading privilege
5. monotone	One unvarying tone

35. pan-all

1. Pan-America	All American
2. panacea	Works for all
3. panorama	Complete view
4. pantheism	All is God
5. panchromatic	Sensitive to all colors

36. path-feeling, suffering

1. apathy	No feelings
2. empathy	In similar feelings
3. pathos	Moving tender emotions
4. sympathy	Similar feelings
5. pathetic	Exciting pity or emotions

37. ped-foot

1. expedite	To put the foot out – make it happen now
2. impede	Put foot in the way – stop, slow down
3. impediment	Something that stands in the way
4. pedal	Device used by foot to create motion
5. pedestrian	One who is traveling by foot

38. phil- love, life

1. audiophile	Lover of music
2. philosophy	Study of the nature & meaning of life
3. philharmonic	Loving music
4. philosopher	One who thinks & speaks of life
5. philology	Loving words & studying languages and the people who speak those languages

39. phob-fear

1. hydrophobia	Fear of water
2. phobia	Unreasonable fear
3. phobic	Fearful
4. acrophobia	Fear of heights
5. technophobia	Fear of technology

40. Phon-sound

1. megaphone	Funnel shaped device for amplifying sound
2. microphone	Device for capturing sound
3. phonetics	Pertaining to sounds
4. phonograph	Player of sounds using records
5. symphony	Similar sounds played together

41. Post-after

1. postdate	To date for a later date
2. posterity	To leave items for those who follow after
3. posthumously	After death; published after death of author
4. post-mortem	Examination of a body after death
5. postpone	To put off until later

42. pre-before

1. preamble	Intro part of discourse
2. precedent	Serving as example previous to current item
3. prejudice	Pre-judging
4. prerequisite	Required beforehand
5. prevent	To keep from happening

43. pro-forward, before, for, forth

1. proceed	To go forward
2. procrastinate	To keep from going forward
3. proponent	One who is for something or someone
4. provide	To give forth
5. provision	To provide for

44. re- back, again

1. recede	To go back
2. revise	To go back to and change
3. revive	To bring back to life
4. recession	To fall back financially
5. revert	To turn back

45. scrib-to write

1. ascribe	To attribute to
2. proscribe	To write out, to doom, to "write off as dead"
3. transcribe	To write over again; to make a written copy
4. subscribe	To write one's signature beneath; to enroll by signing one's signature
5. prescribe	To write or give medical directions

46. script – write/writing

1. conscription	To write or hold for military service
2. manuscript	Hand written document
3. nondescript	Not able to easily describe through writing
4. scripture	Holy writings
5. subscription	Fulfillment according to one writing their signature for

47. spec, spect - to look

1. perspective	One's viewpoint; outlook
2. retrospect	Looking back
3. speculate	To look into the future and predict
4. suspect	To look at as being suspicious
5. inspect	To look into

48. sub-below, under

1. subliminal	Under the surface
2. submerge	To put under
3. submit	To yield to the power of another
4. subservient	To serve as an inferior
5. subterranean	Under the surface of the earth

49. super – over, above

1. superb	Over most; first rate
2. superior	Higher in rank
3. supersonic	At speeds above sound
4. superstructure	A structure built above another
5. supervisor	An overseer

50. syn, sym - same as, similar

1. synonym	A word having the same, or nearly the same, meaning
2. syndrome	A group of symptoms
3. symmetry	Equal proportioned parts
4. sympathy	Feeling similar to another
5. symphony	Similar sounds playing harmoniously

51. tele – far, distant

1. telegraph	A device for conveying the written word at a distance
2. telepathy	Feeling from a distance
3. telephone	A device for transmitting sound at a distance
4. telescope	An instrument used for seeing at a distance
5. television	Seeing images sent over a distance

52. tort – twist, turn

1. contortionist	One who can twist body in incredible ways
2. distort	To twist the truth
3. tortuous	pain inflicted which makes one twist in pain
4. contort	To twist together
5. torture	To inflict pain which makes one twist in pain

53. tri - three

1. triangle	Three angles
2. trilogy	A story in three parts
3. trinity	A representation of God in three personalities
4. triplicate	Three copies
5. tripod	A device with three legs

54. ver – true, truth

1. veracious	Truthful
2. veracity	The state or quality of being true
3. verifiable	Able to prove as true
4. verify	To confirm as true
5. verity	The quality as being true

55. vid, vis – sight, see

1. video	Visual portrayal usually using film
2. videocassette	A cassette that reproduces visual images
3. videoconference	Conference made through using video
4. videogenic	Looking good on video
5. visual	Able to be seen

How many other word parts can you identify that comprise these words?
Highlight, or underline, each word part that was not already mentioned.

Rewrite your words

New word:		Practice writing the new word:		

Rewrite your words

New word:		Practice writing the new word:	

Rewrite your words

New word: **Practice writing the new word:**

Rewrite your words

New word:		Practice writing the new word:	

Rewrite your words

New word:	Practice writing the new word:		

Rewrite your words

New word:		Practice writing the new word:		

Rewrite your words

New word:		Practice writing the new word:		

Rewrite your words

New word:		Practice writing the new word:	

Computer Terminology

Knowing the correct spelling and meaning of the most common computer terms is very important in our technological age. This chapter will start you on the path to computer literacy. Each term is spelled and defined for you.

1. Modem	A device that is connected to another computer through a telephone line or cable.
2. Hard Drive	The drive where most of your information is stored.
3. Software	The programs that may run on your computer.

4. Hardware	Any device attached to the main computer – either internally or externally.
5. Cookies	Contain information that "personalizes" the Web-browsing experience; keep track of where you visit on the web
6. FAQ	Frequently asked questions
7. Favorites	In Internet Explorer, the saved URLs of Web pages you have visited and selected for this folder
8. Home	Button on a Web browser toolbar that allows you to return to your home page, or starting point
9. Inbox	Contains all incoming messages and is one of several mailboxes included in an e-mail program
10. Internet	Large collection of computers all over the world that are connected to one another in various ways
11. File	A saved document
12. Floppy	31/2 inch storage disk
13. Scanner	A device that can scan pictures or pages for use in documents
14. Delete	To erase; the Erase key
15. Shift	Gives you uppercase letters and performs some other functions too

16. Disk Defragmenter	To run software that rearranges your files so that your computer runs better and faster
17. Edit	To make changes to a document
18. Virus	A program infection that can cause trouble in your computer
19. Input	To put in new data, pictures, files, etc.
20. Save	To keep a document or file
21. Network	Created when two or more computers are connected to one another
22. Copy	To create a duplicate
23. Paste	To put copied item into a document
24. Web browser	Software used to locate documents on the Web
25. Insert	To put something into a document
26. Folder	Container of information in Windows that can contain files or other folders
27. Document	One or more pages of information
28. Properties	That which makes up the file, folder, document or hardware of the computer
29. Version	The software edition
30. Web	All of the interconnected computers
31. Undo	To go back to what you previously had

32. Font	The type of lettering and numbering being used in a document
33. Template	A previously created document that can be useful in creating new, similar documents
34. Options	choices
35. World Wide Web	All of the interconnected computers
36. terminology	Language that relates to a certain field of study or area of functioning
37. Customize	To make uniquely yours
38. Attachment	Something, such as a picture or other document, attached to an e-mail
39. Monitor	The screen that you view your computer's information on
40. Merge	To bring information from one source and insert it into a second source – making use of its many features

I. Write each word twice.

1. Modem		
2. Hard Drive		
3. Software		
4. Hardware		
5. Cookies		
6. FAQ		
7. Favorites		
8. Home		
9. Inbox		
10. Internet		
11. File		
12. Floppy		
13. Scanner		
14. Delete		
15. Shift		
16. Disk Defragmenter		
17. Edit		
18. Virus		
19. Input		
20. Save		
21. Network		
22. Copy		
23. Paste		
24. Web browser		
25. Insert		

26. Folder		
27. Document		
28. Properties		
29. Version		
30. Web		
31. Undo		
32. Font		
33. Template		
34. Options		
35. World Wide Web		
36. terminology		
37. Customize		
38. Attachment		
39. Monitor		
40. Merge		

Rewrite your words

New word:	Practice writing the new word:		

Rewrite your words

New word:		Practice writing the new word:	

Chapter 16
Computer Terminology

Across

3. 3 1/2 inch disk

6. to go back to previous condition

7. something added on

8. follow your preferences on the web

12. what you like the most

14. computer devices

15. to make changes

Down

1. to get to uppercase letters

2. drive that stores lots of information

4. choices

5. to make uniquely yours

9. computer programs

10. connects computers

11. computer infection

13. scan a picture with it

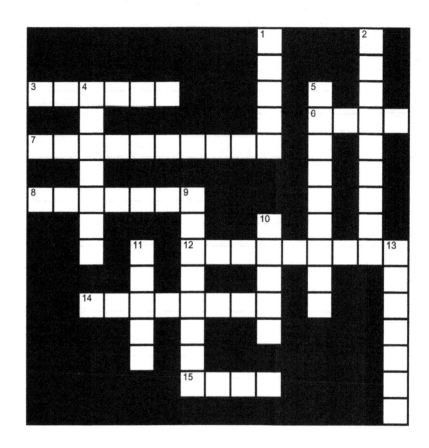

You will probably know most of the meanings for the words in this chapter, but write the definitions for those that are new to you. Additional copies of this form may be printed from the CD that came with this workbook.

Word	Most commonly used definition(s):

You will probably know most of the meanings for the words in this chapter, but write the definitions for those that are new to you. Additional copies of this form may be printed from the CD that came with this workbook.

Word	Most commonly used definition(s):

Rewrite your words

New word:	Practice writing the new word:		